1400+
Chinese Conversational Phrases

Ju Brown, Ph D

⌒⌒

Audio downloads provided at mycjk.com

Library of Congress Control Number: 2007925902
Publisher: BookSurge, LLC
North Charleston, South Carolina

To order additional copies, please contact us.
BookSurge, LLC
www.booksurge.com
1-866-308-6235

Introduction

Chinese can be a demanding language to learn. This is partly due to the fact that Chinese is not a phonetic language. Speaking Chinese is not related in any way to writing Chinese. All beginners, including native Chinese speakers, learn speaking and writing separately. This can prove challenging for most of us only familiar with phonetic languages, but it can also make the Chinese language a more interesting language to learn. If you follow how its characters are made up and their meanings underneath, your learning experience will be much easier.

Considering China's economic power, and 5000 years of cultural heritage, learning Chinese today can be a rewarding experience. To begin learning Chinese, there are a few basic things you need to know that will make the process much more fun and easy. We will begin with some basic rules everyone learning Chinese must be familiar with. As you go through the over 1400 phrases in this book you may need to refresh yourself from time to time with these basic components of the language. Whatever your motivation may be for learning Chinese, this book will help you learn the basics and daily conversations. Be sure to listen to the real pronunciation.

This book consists of phrases by situations. The basic format (with the exception of Signs) is:

Engligh
Hanyu Pinyin, Chinese characters

Explanations are added as needed. MORE sections carry many different words you can apply to real conversations. The 2008 Beijing Olympics section is included as a special appendix.

The Characteristics of Chinese Language

Chinese belongs to the Sino-Tibetan family of languages. About one-fifth of the people in the world speak some form of Chinese as their native language. Even though many dialects of Chinese are so different they are mutually unintelligible, they are all classified as one Chinese language. The official language of government and education in the People's Republic of China is called Putonghua 普通话 (means the common speech), which is based on Beijing-area Mandarin. Mandarin, the official language in Taiwan, is called Guoyu 國語. Mandarin is called Huayu 华语 in South East Asia, where many overseas Chinese reside.

Since there is no alphabet in the Chinese language, the principles of the Hanyu Pinyin 汉语拼音 (means Chinese spell sound) system is used as an oral representation of Chinese characters. This is the basis for creating the Latin script reading of a character, and represents the spoken sounds of Putonghua. This book will follow the Hanyu Pinyin system. Hanyu Pinyin is very helpful in guessing how to pronounce the word as well as reading signs on the streets in China. For example, many Post Offices have signs with Pinyin instead of the English translation like this:

Post Office →
邮局
You Ju

While there are many spoken dialects in Chinese, there is only one written Chinese. The Chinese written language is of an old and conservative type that assigns a single distinctive symbol, or character, to each word in the vocabulary. Each character represents a word or idea rather than a sound. In the mid 1950s, the Chinese government simplified some 2000 of the most frequently used characters in an effort to popularize literacy. Today, China and Singapore use these "Simplified Chinese" characters called Jianti Zi 简体字 (literally means simple-style-characters), and Taiwan uses "Traditional Chinese" characters called Fanti Zi 繁體字 (literally means complicated-style-characters). Hong Kong and Macao still use Traditional Chinese but are adopting more and more Simplified ones. This book will solely use Simplified Chinese based on Putonghua standard.

Meaning	Pronunciation	Traditional Chinese	Simplified Chinese
Son	ér	兒	儿
Door	mén	門	门
Horse	mǎ	馬	马

Let's look at some characteristics of the Chinese language.

- Chinese is monosyllabic and each individual character represents an idea or thing. Chinese often uses combinations of monosyllables to express different meanings. Today there is a trend of more and more polysyllabic words forming.
- Chinese is an isolating language, which means it depends on word order and structure. Chinese doesn't change its word through inflection like English. To indicate aspect and mood, Chinese use heavy particles. Common particles are explained in this book.
- Chinese is a tonal language and the variance in pitch creates a different representation of meaning to the listener. Tone is extremely important in Chinese, as the same pronunciation with different tones can mean totally different things, and when you say Chinese without proper tones, you may not be understood at all. For example, if shui jiao is said

both in 4th tones, it is written like this 睡觉, meaning sleep. When shui jiao is said both in 3rd tones, it is written like this水饺, meaning dumplings. The good news is Putonghua has only 4 tones, not like the Cantonese dialect which has 9 tones!!

- Chinese is a topic-prominent language, which organizes its syntax to make sentences "topic-comment structured", where the topic is the thing being talked about (predicated), and the comment is what is said about the topic. This structure is independent of the syntactic ordering of SVO (subject + verb+ object), and may be marked by mentioning the topic first in the sentence and then the comment.
- Chinese is a null subject language that has an independent clause which lacks an explicit subject. Pronouns can be dropped as well when they are understood. In this book, you will see many pronouns that are not exactly translated into Chinese.
- Chinese does not have tenses. There are, however, words to indicate the passage of time, days, and change, such as tomorrow, now, and so forth.
- Chinese does not use grammatical gender.
- Chinese has an extensive measure word system. In Chinese, simple numerals cannot quantify a noun itself, and a measure word <u>must be</u> used between numerals and nouns. Some measure words are used to quantify verbs to indicate the amount of time. Measure words are explained as they appear.
- Chinese use a lot of traditional idiomatic expressions, even in daily conversations. These idiomatic expressions usually consist of four characters, and there are said to be over 5000 common ones. The Chinese like to coin new phrases, especially slogans with 4 characters.

Hanyu Pinyin

Consonants

b	p	m	f
d	t	n	l
g	k	h	
j	q	x	
zh	ch	sh	r
z	c	s	

Chinese has 21 consonants and most of them in Pinyin are generally pronounced as in English with few exceptions. Here are different pronunciations you will need to look out for.

q: "ch" as in "cheek"

x: "sh" as in "she"

zh: "zh" with slightly rolled tip of the tongue

ch: "ch" with slightly rolled tip of the tongue

sh: "sh" with slightly rolled tip of the tongue

z: "ds" as in "kids". It feels like the tip of the tongue touches the back of the front teeth.

c: "ts" as in "cats". It feels like the tip of the tongue touches the back of the front teeth.

s: s sound with the feeling like the tip of the tongue touches the back of the front teeth.

Vowels

	i	u	ü
a	ia (ya)	ua (wa)	
o		uo (wo)	
e	ie (ye)		üe (yue)
(s-)i, (sh-)i			
er			
ai		uai (wai)	
ei		uei (wei)	
ao	iao (yao)		
ou	iou (you, -iu)		
an	ian (yan)	uan (wan)	üan (yuan)
en	ien (yen, -in)	uen (wen)	üen (yun)
ang	iang (yang)	uang (wang)	
eng	ieng (ying, -ing)	ueng (weng)	üeng (yong)
ong	iong		

The basic vowels - a, e, i, o, and u - are generally pronounced as they are <u>in Italian, German, and Spanish</u> rather than in English.

a: "a" as in "father"

e: "u" as in "up"

i: sounds "ee". "i" is silent when preceded by "c", "ch", "r", "s", "sh", "z" or "zh".

o: plain "o"

u: "oo" as in "cool"

ü: as in German "ü". Say "ee" with rounded lips

en: as in taken.

ie: ye as in yet.

ian (yan): as **i** + **ê** + **n**; like English **yen.**

ui: as **u** + **ei**. The i is pronounced like ei.

üan (yuan): as **ü** + **ê**+ **n**

There are also a few rules about writing vowels in the Pinyin system:
- w is placed before syllables starting with u.
- y is placed before syllables starting with i and ü.
- ü is written as u when there is no ambiguity (such as ju, qu, and xu), but written as ü when there are corresponding u syllables (such as lü and nü) .

Pinyin words with single meaning, which is a set of 2 or more characters, or words combined of two words with one meaning are usually written together without spaces. Verbs and their suffixes (-zhe, -le and -guo) are written as one. Duplicated characters (AA) are written together, but two characters duplicated (ABAB) are written separated.
Words with four or more characters having one meaning are split up with their original meanings if possible. A proper noun is capitalized.

Tones

Chinese has 4 tones and a neutral tone. Don't let these tones intimidate you. Let's imagine these tones in musical notes that are 5 levels of your voice. Just add little ups and downs in your normal memorizing process.

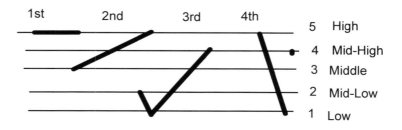

Tone	Pronunciation	Mark Examples
1st Tone	5-5 Start High and finish High	mā (a macron on the vowel)
2nd Tone	3-5 Start middle and finish High	má (an acute accent on the vowel)
3rd Tone	2-1-4 Start Mid-Low, go down to Low and go up to Mid-High. Half 3rd tone is Mid-Low to Low.	mǎ (a reverse circumflex on the vowel)
4th Tone	5-1 Start High and finish Low	mà (a grave accent on the vowel)
5th (Neutral) Tone	4 Mid-High	ma (a normal vowel without any accent mark)

When there is more than one vowel, the tone mark appears on the first vowel. However, when the first vowel is i, u or ü, then the tone mark appears on the second vowel. (y and w are not considered vowels for these rules.)

Tones are designed for learners to learn Chinese easily. Apparently, when Chinese native speakers speak Chinese, they are not aware of any tones. There are also variations for the characters to change their tones in some circumstances. However, these rules are very few and easy to follow. These changes happen for easier pronunciation after all!!

1. 3rd tone+ 3rd tone= 2nd tone + 3rd tone
When a 3 rd tone comes before a 3rd tone, first 3rd tone becomes a second tone.

2. 3rd tone+ 1, 2, 4 or neutral tone= half 3rd tone + 1, 2, 4 or neutral tone
When a 3 rd tone comes before 1, 2, 4 or neutral tone, first 3rd tone becomes a half 3rd tone.

3. Yī 一 (one 1), qī 七 (seven 7), bā 八 (eight 8) , bù 不 + 4th tone= yí 一, qí 七, bá 八, bú 不 + 4th tone
This is called "yīqībābù 一七八不" tone change. This is one of the few important tone changes to memorize. yīqībābù 一七八不 are originally first tones. However they are pronounced as a second tone when followed by a fourth tone.

4. Yī 一 (one 1) + 1st, 2nd , 3rd tone= yì 一 + 1st, 2nd , 3rd tone.
When yī 一 is followed by 1st, 2nd , or 3rd tone it becomes a 4th tone.

5. Yī 一 and bù 不 become neutral tones between the same words.

Writing Chinese

The Chinese writing system is believed to have developed more than 4000 years ago and the use of pictographs has remained relatively intact with few changes over the centuries. Chinese writing consists of an individual character or ideogram for every syllable.

Chinese characters usually take up the same amount of space, and each character is roughly the same size and proportion. Since the characters fit into a square space, Chinese call them fangkuaizi 方块字, which literally means "square-block-characters". A Chinese word or phrase, called ci 词, is composed of one or more characters of zi 字. Zi is the minimum meaningful character in Chinese. Dictionaries have words or phrases called cidian 词典 and individual characters are called zidian 字典. There are no spaces used when ci is written in Pinyin.

Each character also has at least one fundamental component called a "radical". Radicals are called bushou 部首, which literally means part and initial. A radical carries a defined meaning itself when it is used alone, and can be combined with other radicals to form compound characters. There are 214 commonly recognized radicals in Chinese. Recognizing these radicals can be a big help in understanding the structure of Chinese characters. Chinese dictionaries are arranged in order of their radicals, and the total number of strokes. For example, the character shuǐ 水, meaning water, is written 氵 as a radical. Therefore, the following words are all water related: zhī 汁 (juice), jiāng 江 (river), qì 泣 (weep), tāng 汤 (soup).

The traditional Chinese language had no punctuation at all when it was written, including poetry and calligraphy. Punctuation marks came into use only recently in China, which is different from Western punctuation.

- Spaces are normally not used between words in Chinese.
- The Chinese full stop (or period) is a small circle (。).
- Exclamation marks (!), question marks (?), colons (:), semi colons (;) and parentheses ( ) are the same as Western ones, but a little larger and take up a bigger space.

Writing Chinese can be difficult. Chinese characters look very complicated, and almost look like a picture. Writing Chinese is an important part of the step by step process in learning Chinese. Understanding basic strokes and radicals can help in understanding the whole structure of each character. Many complicated looking characters are actually made up of several separate parts, each delivering different meanings.

Chinese basic strokes are:

	Chinese Name	How to write	Example
一	Heng (horizontal)	rightward stroke	一
丨	Shu (vertical)	downward stroke	十
丶	Dian (dot)	tiny dash	字
丿	Ti (rise)	flick up and rightwards	习
乀	Na (press down)	falling rightwards (fattening at the bottom)	人
丿	Pie (throw away)	falling leftwards (with slight curve)	千

亅	Shugou (vertical and hook)	downward stroke and appended to other strokes	小
ㄴ	Shuzhe (vertical and break)	downward stroke and turn 90°	它

Chinese characters are usually written following some basic rules. The strokes should be written in the right order and in the right way.

- Write from left to right and from top to bottom.
- Horizontal before vertical.
- Cutting strokes through a character are written last.
- Diagonals are written right-to-left before left-to-right.
- Vertical center strokes are written before vertical or diagonal outside strokes.
- Outside enclosing strokes are written before inside strokes; bottom strokes are written last. Left vertical strokes are written before enclosing strokes.
- Dots and minor strokes are last.

There are many books and websites including mycjk.com you can learn the right order of writing Chinese characters. Here are some samples.

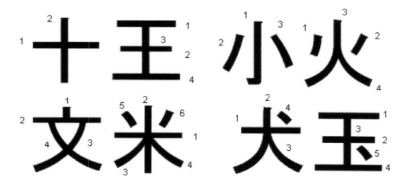

Table of Contents

 **Common Greetings**

🎧1. Hi/ hello/ how are you/ how do you do?
Nǐ hǎo 你好?
- Nǐ hǎo 你好 can be used anytime of the day. You can also say it as an answer in return.
- The left part of nǐ 你, 亻 is from the radical 人. 亻 is used to describe a person. You can guess any characters with 亻 on the left as having something to do with people.
- Nǐ 你 and hǎo 好 are both 3rd tones. Say nǐ 你 as a second tone.

🎧2. Hi/ hello/ how are you/ how do you do?
Nín hǎo 您好? (Honorific form)
- Nín 您 is an honorific form of ni 你. The difference is the character "heart" xīn 心 added to the bottom to make the honorific word 您. 你+心=您

🎧3. Good morning!
Zǎo 早!

🎧4. Good afternoon!
Wǔ ān 午安!

5. Good evening!
Wǎn ān 晚安!

 MORE: Greetings around the Clock
Good morning: nǐ zǎo 你早, zǎo ān 早安, zǎoshang hǎo 早上好, zǎochén hǎo 早晨好, shàngwǔ hǎo 上午好
Good afternoon: xiàwǔ hǎo 下午好
Good evening: wǎnshang hǎo 晚上好

🎧6. Hello everyone?
Dàjiā hǎo 大家好?

MORE: Saying Hello
Hǎo 好 can be added after someone's name or title to make general greetings.
Hello: nǐmen hǎo 你们好? (to more than one person)
Hello teacher : lǎoshī hǎo 老师好?
Hello manager Zhang : Zhāng jīnglǐ hǎo 张经理好?

🎧7. I am doing well, how about you?
Wǒ hěn hǎo 我很好, nǐ ne 你呢?
- Wǒ hěn hǎo 我很好 is three 3rd tones in a row. Since hěn hǎo 很好 are related to each other (adverb and adjective), read it as half 3rd + 2nd + 3rd format. When a 3rd tone is followed by a neutral tone, as in nǐ ne 你呢, nǐ 你 becomes half 3rd tone as well.

8. I'm fine too.
Wǒ yě hěn hǎo 我也很好。

🎧9. Long time no see.
Hǎo jiǔ bú jiàn 好久不见。
- Bù 不 is originally a 4th tone, but it becomes 2nd tone before a 4th tone.

🎧10. How's it going?
Zěnme yàng 怎么样?
- This is used between close relationships.

11. How have you been doing lately?
Zuìjìn zěnme yàng 最近怎么样?

12. I've been doing pretty well.
Tǐng hǎo de 挺好的。

13. How's everything?
Yíqiè hái hǎo ba 一切还好吧?

14. It's going pretty well.
Yíqiè hěn shùnlì 一切很顺利。

15. I've been alright.
Hái búcuò 还不错。

MORE: Bù 不

Bù 不 is one of the most important characters in the Chinese language. It is an adverb used to form negative words and sentences. It is also used as " no" to questions.

Hǎo 好 (good) ↔ bù hǎo 不好 (bad)
Kěnéng 可能 (possible) ↔ bù kěnéng 不可能 (impossible)
Kāixīn 开心 (happy) ↔ bù kāixīn 不开心 (not happy)
Jiàn 见 (see, meet) ↔ bú jiàn 不见 (don't see)

🎧16. Same as always.
Hé píngcháng yíyàng 和平常一样。

17. How's work?
Gōngzuò zěnme yàng 工作怎么样?

18. How was work today?
Jīintiān gōngzuò zěnme yàng 今天工作怎么样?

19. How did it go today?
Jīintiān zěnme yàng 今天怎么样?

🎧20. So-so.
Hái còuhé ba 还凑合吧。

21. Pretty good.
Hái kěyǐ 还可以。

22. So far，So good.
Mùqián hái búcuò 目前还不错。
- Bù 不 is originally 4th tone, but it becomes 2nd tone when it's followed by a 4th tone.

23. How's your family?
Nǐde jiārén zěnme yàng 你的家人怎么样?
- De 的 is a particle indicating attributes after a noun, pronoun, verb, or adjective, and is omitted in many occasions. For example, I or me in Chinese is wǒ 我, and wǒde 我的 means "my".

24. Everyone's fine.
Dàjiā dōu hěn hǎo 大家都很好。
- Hǎo 好 means good and is usually used with an adverb of degree to indicate "how" good it is. Hěn 很 is the most frequently used adverb, especially with mono-syllabic adjectives such as hǎo 好. Hěn 很 also loses its own independent meaning of value, and sometimes it doesn't really intensify the degree of an adjective.

25. Are you healthy?
Nǐ shēntǐ hǎo ma? 你身体好吗?
- Asking someone if they are healthy or not may sound strange unless you are visiting a sick person, but this is a common Chinese greeting, especially to elderly people.

26. Have you eaten?
Nǐ chī fàn le ma 你吃饭了吗?
- This is one of the most common greetings in China, especially around lunch or dinner time. Answers to this question are always positive, whether the person has eaten or not!!!

27. I did eat, how about you?
Wǒ chī le 我吃了, nǐ ne 你呢?

28. I already ate.

Wǒ chīguo le 我吃过了。

- Guo 过 - a particle indicating completion of action as an experience.

🎧29. Are you busy at work?

Nǐ gōngzuò máng ma 你工作忙吗?

- Ma 吗 is an interrogative particle used at the end of a declarative sentence to form a question.

🎧30. I'm really busy now.

Wǒ xiànzài zhēnde hěn máng 我现在真的很忙。

> **MORE: Busy**
> I am busy : Wǒ máng 我忙.
> I am not busy: Wǒ bù máng 我不忙.
> I am pretty busy : Wǒ hěn máng 我很忙.
> I am too busy : Wǒ tài máng 我太忙.
> I am not very busy : Wǒ bú tài máng 我不太忙.
> I am not very busy lately: Wǒ zuìjìn bú tài máng 我最近不太忙.
> I am not very busy, how about you?: Wǒ bú tài máng, nǐ ne 我不太忙, 你呢?

31. What have you been doing?

Máng shénme ne 忙什么呢?

- Ne 呢 a postposition used at the end of the interrogative sentence

32. Just working.

Shàng bān bei 上班呗。

- bei 呗 is a postposition indicating that the idea is simple and easy to understand.

🎧33. Nothing much.

Méi máng shénme 没忙什么。

Thanks, sorry, excuse me and OK

🎧34. Thank you.
Xièxiè 谢谢。

35. Thanks a lot.
Duōxiè 多谢。

🎧36. Thank you very much.
Fēicháng gǎnxiè 非常感谢。

37. Thank you for helping me.
Xièxiè nǐde bāngzhù
谢谢你的帮助。

38. Thank you for everything.
Gǎnxiè nǐ zuòde yíqiè
感谢你做的一切。

🎧39. Thanks for telling me.
Xièxiè nǐ gàosù wǒ 谢谢你告诉我。

40. Thanks for the warning.
Xièxiè nǐde tíxǐng 谢谢你的提醒。

41. Thank you for your cooperation.
Xièxiè hézuò 谢谢合作。

42. No matter what, I need to thank you.
Bùguǎn zěn yàng, háishì yào xièxiè nǐ
不管怎样, 还是要谢谢你。

🎧43. Thank you for the trouble you've taken for me.
Máfán nǐ le 麻烦你了。

🎧44. You are welcome.
Bú (yòng) xiè 不(用)谢。

45. It's my pleasure.
Lèyì wèi nǐ xiàoláo 乐意为您效劳。

🎧46. Don't mention it.
Bú kèqi 不客气。
- Literally kè 客 means guest and qì 气 means air or manners as in kèqi 客气. Kèqi 客气 is a very important term in Chinese social and business life. It not only means courteous, considerate, polite, and well-mannered, but also represents humbleness and modesty. The word bú kèqi 不客气 would translate as "you don't have to be so humble or courteous", but now it means you are welcome in response to thank you.

47. It's nothing.
Xiǎo shìqíng 小事情。

48. Don't mention it.
Bùzú guàchǐ 不足挂齿。

🎧49. It's no big deal.
Zhè méi shénme dàbuliǎo de 这没什么大不了的。
- Dàbuliǎo 大不了 is mostly used in a negative sentence, meaning serious.

50. It isn't much.
Zhèshì wēi bùzú dào de 这是微不足道的。

51. I am sorry.
Bù hǎoyìsi 不好意思。

🎧52. I am sorry.

Duìbuqǐ 对不起。

- Duìbuqǐ 对不起 means I am sorry, excuse me, and pardon me. Its meaning can be pretty serious and formal based on the occasion.

53. Sorry to have kept you waiting.

Duìbuqǐ, ràng nǐ jiǔ děng le 对不起, 让你久等了。

- Ràng 让 is a preposition used in a passive sentence to introduce the agent.

54. Sorry, I am late.

Zhēn bàoqiàn, wǒ lái wǎn le 真抱歉, 我来晚了。

🎧55. I am so sorry for you.

Wǒ zhēn wèi nǐ nánguò 我真为你难过。

🎧56. That's all right.

Méi guānxi 没关系。

- Méi 没 is another negative adverb, but is mainly used to negate yǒu 有, meaning there is, or there are. The shorter form méi 没, instead of méiyǒu 没有, is common as well. Méi guānxi 没关系 is also said as méiyǒu guānxi 没有关系。

MORE: About guānxi 关系
It means relationships, but is now more often referred to as "connections" which is one of the most important Chinese social terms. Guānxi 关系 is a personal connection between two people in which one is able to prevail upon another to perform a favor or service. In many occasions personal or business relationships in China depend on guānxi 关系.

🎧57. That's all right.

Méi shénme 没什么。

🎧58. Never mind.
Bú yàojǐn 不要紧。

🎧59. No Problem!
Méi wèntí 没问题。

60. That's not a problem.
Nà méi wèntí 那没问题。

61. This seems all right.
Kànlái zhè méi wèntí 看来这没问题。
- Kànlái 看来 means it seems, or it appears. Another common one for the same meaning is kànyàngzi 看样子.

🎧62. I didn't mean it.
Wǒ bú shì gùyì de 我不是故意的。

63. It slipped my mind.
Wǒ bù liúshén wàng le 我不留神忘了。

64. Please accept my apology.
Qǐng jiēshòu wǒde dàoqiàn 请接受我的道歉。

65. Please don't blame yourself.
Qǐng búyào zéguài nǐ zìjǐ 请不要责怪你自己。
- Yào 要 is one of the most important verbs, which has such meanings as need, want, must, or it can mean going to, such as in "it's going to rain".. With bù 不, búyào 不要 becomes an adverb meaning "don't".

🎧66. I apologize.
Wǒ hěn bàoqiàn 我很抱歉。

🎧67. I feel terrible about it.

Tài duìbuqǐ le 太对不起了。

68. I hope you'll forgive me.
Wǒ xīwàng nǐ néng yuánliàng wǒ 我希望你能原谅我。

🎧69. I beg your pardon.
Qǐng nǐ yuánliàng 请你原谅。

🎧70. I beg your pardon?
Qǐng nín zài shuō yí biàn 请您再说一遍。
- • Biàn 遍 is a measure word indicating the process of an action from beginning to end.

🎧71. Excuse me
Qǐngwèn 请问。

72. Is it OK?
Hǎo bu hǎo 好不好?

73. Of course!
Dāngrán le 当然了。

74. OK!
Hǎo 好!

🎧75. That's good.
Hěn hǎo 很好。

76. That's great.
Hǎo jí le 好极了。

🎧77. It's wonderful.
Zhēn búcuò 真不错。

🎧78. Great!
Tài bàng le 太棒了。

🎧79. That couldn't be better.
Nà zài hǎo búguò le 那再好不过了。
- Búguò 不过 is used after an adjective to form the superlative degree.

80. It's very kind of you!
Nǐ zhēn shì tài hǎo le 你真是太好了。
- Le 了 is one of most difficult particles in the Chinese language, which indicates the work is completed or a change has been made. Since the Chinese language doesn't have tenses, and le 了 involves completion meaning, many people misunderstand le 了 as a particle to form past tenses. To complicate things more, le 了 can be used in future tenses as well. For example: I'll go when I am done eating. Wǒ chī wán le jiù qù 我吃完了就去 (wán 完- use up, run out, jiù 就- right away, qù 去-go). In this sentence, even though le 了 is used, eating hasn't finished yet.

First Time Meeting People

81. I'll introduce.
Wǒ jièshào yíxià 我介绍一下。
- Yíxià 一下 is used after a verb to indicate something happening briefly.

🎧82. This is my friend.
Zhè shì wǒde péngyou 这是我的朋友。

🎧83. Nice to meet you.
Rènshi nǐ hěn gāoxìng
认识你很高兴。

84. Nice to meet you too.
Rènshi nǐ wǒ yě hěn gāoxìng
认识你我也很高兴 。

85. Glad to see you.
Hěn gāoxìng jiàndào nǐ 很高兴见到你。

86. I'm glad to see you again.
Hěn gāoxìng yòu jiàndào nǐ 很高兴又见到你。

87 Nice talking with you.
Hěn gāoxìng hé nǐ shuōhuà 很高兴和你说话。

88. Please write down your name.
Qǐng xiě xià nǐde xìngmíng
请写下你的姓名。

89. Please fill out the form.
Qǐng tián zhè zhāng biǎo 请填这张表。

90. What's your name?
Nǐ jiào shénme míngzi 你叫什么名字?

- The Chinese name is made up of a family name xìng 姓, which is always placed first, followed by the personal or given name míng 名 or míngzi 名字. The majority of Chinese family names have only one character, but there are a few with two. Chinese given names usually have one or two characters as well.

91. What's your last name?
Nǐ xìng shénme 你姓什么?

92. May I ask your last name?
Nín guì xìng 您贵姓? (Polite way)

- Since many different Chinese characters can be pronounced in the exact same way, Chinese people often state which words their names are found in when telling each other their names.

93. My last name is Zhang, called Zhang Ming.
Wŏ xìng Zhāng, jiào Zhāng Míng 我姓张, 叫张明。

MORE: Examples of stating Chinese names
My last name is Zhang, gong chang Zhang.
Wŏ xìng Zhāng, gōng cháng zhāng 我姓张, 弓长张。
My last name is Li, mu zi Li.
Wŏ xìng Lĭ, mù zĭ Lĭ. 我姓李, 木子李。
A popular given name for the girl lì 丽 is explained as lì 丽 of měilì 美丽, meaning beautiful. Yīng 英 character is usually explained as yīng 英 of yīngjùn 英俊, meaning handsome, or yīng 英 of yīngguó 英国, meaning England.

94. My name is Tom.
Wŏ jiào Tāngmŭ 我叫汤姆。

- Names of foreigners are usually transliterated based on their pronunciation. Although characters are chosen for their sound, good meanings are considered as well. Exceptions are Japanese and Korean names which already have Chinese characters that Chinese read in their own Chinese pronunciation. For example: the Japanese last name Toyoda 丰田 is read as fēng tián (fēng 丰- abundant, tián 田-field) .

MORE: Examples of American names in Chinese
John : Yuē hàn 约翰 (yuē 约-simple, hàn 翰-brush)
Chris: Kè lĭ sī 克里斯 (kè 克-overcome, lĭ 里-town, sī 斯-gentle)
Mark : Mă kè 马克 (mă 马-horse, kè 克-overcome)
Mike: Mài kè 麦克 (mài 麦-wheat, kè 克-overcome)
Scott: Sī kē tè 斯科特 (sī 斯-gentle, kē 科-family, tè 特-special)
Bill: Bĭ ěr 比尔 (bĭ 比-compare, ěr 尔-you)
Jeff: Jié fū 杰夫 (jié 杰-outstanding, fū 夫-man)
Jane: Jiăn 简 (jiăn 简-simple)
Susan : Sū shān 苏珊 (sū 苏-come to, shān 珊-coral)
Diana: Dài ān nà 戴安娜 (dài 戴-put on, ān 安-peaceful, nà 娜-pretty)

95. Do you speak Chinese?

Nǐ huì shuō hànyǔ ma 你会说汉语吗?

- Along with hànyǔ 汉语, zhōngwén 中文 is also commonly used for Chinese language.

96. I can (speak Chinese).

Wǒ huì (shuō hànyǔ) 我会(说汉语)。

MORE: Languages
English : Yīngyǔ 英语 or Yīngwén 英文
Japanese : Rìyǔ 日语 or Rìwén 日文
French: Fǎyǔ 法语 or Fǎwén 法文
German: Déyǔ 德语 or Déwén 德文
Spanish: Xībānyáyǔ 西班牙语 or Xībānyáwén 西班牙文

97. I can't (speak Chinese).

Wǒ bú huì (shuō hànyǔ) 我不会(说汉语)。

98. I can speak a little (Chinese).

Wǒ huì shuō yìdiǎnr (hànyǔ) 我会说一点儿(汉语)。

- When you say yìdiǎnr 一点儿, "n" pronunciation is dropped and roll your tongue as you normally say "r" at the end.

99. How long have you studied Chinese?

Nǐ xué hànyǔ xuéle duō jiǔ 你学汉语学了多久?

- This question might look a little complicated, but think of it as two sentences combined into one: nǐ xué hànyǔ 你学汉语 (you study Chinese) + xué le duōjiǔ 学了多久 (how long have you studied). The formula is: subject + verb + object + verb + le 了 + duō jiǔ 多久

100. You speak Chinese like a native.

Nǐ shuō hànyǔ xiàng ge běndì rén
你说汉语像个本地人。

101. Not at all!

Bùgǎndāng, bùgǎndāng 不敢当, 不敢当。
- • It's a polite expression in reply to a compliment. It literally means I wish I could deserve your compliment.

102. Is this your first time in China?
Nǐ dì yí cì lái zhōngguó ma 你第一次来中国吗?

103. This is my 3rd time.
Zhè shì dì sān cì 这是第三次。

104. Where are you from?
Nǐ shì nǎli rén 你是哪里人?

105. I'm from the USA.
Wǒ shì Měiguó rén 我是美国人。

106. Are you American?
Nǐ shì Měiguó rén ma 你是美国人吗?

 MORE: Country names in Chinese

England: Yīngguó 英国

Germany: Déguó 德国

France: Fǎguó 法国

Mongolia: Ménggǔ 蒙古

Russia: Sūlián 苏联

Japan: Rìběn 日本

Korea: Hánguó 韩国

Thailand: Tàiguó 泰国

Singapore: Xīngjiāpō 星加坡

Malaysia: Mǎláixīyà 马来西亚

Vietnam: Yuènán 越南

Mexico: Mòxīgē 墨西哥

Australia: Àozhōu 澳洲

New Zealand: Xīnxīlán 新西兰

107. No, I'm a Canadian.
Bù, wǒ shì Jiānádà rén 不，我是加拿大人。

108. What do you do for a living?
Nǐ zuò shénme gōngzuò 你做什么工作?

109. Where do you work?
Nǐ zài nǎli gōngzuò 你在哪里工作?
- Zài 在 is a verb meaning exist or indicating the position of a person or thing. In this question, zài 在 is used as a preposition indicating place.

110. Are you married?
Nǐ jiéhūnle ma 你结婚了吗?
- It might be a very personal and private question in Western culture, but it is a common one in Chinese culture. Chinese married women usually retain their maiden name as their family name.

111. I am married.
Wǒ jiéhūn le 我结婚了。

112. I am not married yet.
Wǒ hái méiyǒu jiéhūn 我还没有结婚。

113. I was married.
Wǒ jiéguo hūn 我结过婚。

114. How old are you? (To the same age person)
Nǐ jīnnián duō dà 你今年多大?

MORE: Year	
Last year : qùnián 去年	
This year : jīnnián 今年	
Next year: míngnián 明年	
Next next year: hòunián 后年	

115. How old are you? (To someone younger)
Nǐ jīnnián jǐ suì 你今年几岁？

116. How old are you? (To someone older)
Nín jīnnián duōdà suìshu 您今年多大岁数?

117. Where do you live?
Nǐ zhù nǎr 你住哪儿?

118. I live in Shanghai.
Wǒ zhù zài Shànghǎi 我住在上海。

119. I live on Zhonghua street.
Wǒ zhù zài Zhōnghuá lù 我住在中华路。

120. This is my address.
Zhè shì wǒde dìzhǐ 这是我的地址。

> **MORE: Address**
> Along with dìzhǐ 地址, zhùzhǐ 住址 is another common term for address. In China, address is always written from the big unit to the small unit, and a person's name is last on the envelope.
> Province-city-district-road-unit number
> Zip code
> Name

121. What's your phone number?
Nǐde diànhuà hàomǎ duōshao 你的电话号码多少?

- Jǐ 几 and duōshao 多少 are both used to ask about numbers. Jǐ 几 is usually asked for a question that has small numbers, usually less than 10. Duōshao 多少 can be used for any numbers, large or small. Jǐ 几 is usually followed by a measure word, but duōshao 多少 can be used alone.

122. My phone number is 335-7798.

Sān sān wǔ qī qī jiǔ bā 三三五七七九八。

- Read each phone number one by one.

123. Do you have an email address?

Nǐ yǒu diànzi yóujiàn dìzhǐ ma
你有电子邮件地址吗?

124. Yes, my email address is xxx@xxxx.com

Yǒu, wǒde diànzi yóujiàn dìzhǐ shì xxx@xxxx.com
有, 我的电子邮件地址是 xxx@xxxx.com 。

(@ is read as quān 圈, and • is diǎn 点.)

MORE: Internet related terms
In Chinese, foreign words are either transliterated according to its pronunciation, or translated based on its meaning, or the combination of both.

Email: diànzi yóujiàn 电子邮件 (translation meaning electronic mail)
Internet: yīntè wǎng 因特网 (transliteration for " Inter" yīntè 因特 & translation for wǎng 网 meaning "net".)
Internet address: yīntè wǎng dìzhǐ 因特网地址 (wǎng zhǐ 网址 for short.)
Email Box: (diànzi) yóuxiāng (电子) 邮箱 (xiāng 箱–box)

 **Saying Goodbye**

125. Good bye. / See you./ So long.

Zàijiàn 再见。

- The exact literal meaning is see you again, but you can say zàijiàn 再见 regardless of seeing that person again.

126. Bye-bye!

Bài bai 拜拜!

- This is a direct transliteration from bye-bye, and often used by younger generations.

127. Bye (and walk slow)!
Màn zǒu 慢走!
- It literally translates to walk slowly. When it's said to someone who leaves, it includes the further meaning of walk in peace or be careful. Màn 慢 is often used twice to emphasize its meaning of slowly or gradually as well, such as mànmànr zǒu 慢慢儿走.

128. See you later.
Yǐhòu jiàn 以后见!

129. See you around.
Huítóu jiàn 回头见!

130. It's getting late.
Tiān bù zǎo le 天不早了。
- Zǎo 早 is used as a good morning greeting and for morning itself. Here it is used as an adjective meaning early.

131. Let's go home.
Wǒmen huíjiā ba 我们回家吧。

132. Time to go.
Gāi zǒu le 该走了。

133. Time has come.
Dào shíjiān le 到时间了。

134. Time is up.
Méiyǒu shíjiān le 没有时间了。

135. It's about time.
Wǒ kàn shíjiān chābuduō le 我看时间差不多了。

- Chābuduō 差不多 means just about right (enough) or not bad. It is also a common answer when someone doesn't want to say anything for sure.

136. I have to go.
Wǒ děi gàocí le 我得告辞了。
- When 得 is used as a verb, read it as děi. It means need, must, or have to.

137. Can't you stay a little longer?
Zài dāi huìr ba 再呆会儿吧!
- Ba 吧 is used at the end of a sentence to indicate suggestion.

138. I'll stop by later.
Wǒ huì shùnbiàn lái de 我会顺便来的。

139. I'm here to say good bye.
Wǒ lái xiàng nǐ gàobié 我来向你告别。

140. I don't know what to say.
Wǒ bù zhīdào shuō shénme hǎo
我不知道说什么好。
- Without hǎo 好, you can also just say wǒ bù zhīdào shuō shénme 我不知道 说什么. But with hǎo 好 at the end of a sentence it emphasizes what is "appropriate" to say.
- Compared this to " I don't know what you are talking about " wǒ bù zhīdào nǐ shuō shénme 我不知道你说什么. In this sentence, the subjects of zhīdào 知道 and shuō 说 are different.

141. Don't work too hard.
Bié gànde tài měng 别干得太猛。

142. Take care.
Qǐng duō bǎozhòng 请多保重。

🎧 143. Let's keep in touch.
Bǎochí liánluò 保持联络。

144. Please drop me a line.
Qǐng gěi wǒ xiě xìn 请给我写信。
- Gěi 给 means for, to. It's a preposition introducing the object of one's service

🎧 145. I'll write you (a letter).
Wǒ huì gěi nǐ xiě xìn de 我会给你写信的。

146. Don't forget to write.
Bié wàng le xiě xìn 别忘了写信。

🎧 147. I won't.
Wàng bu liǎo 忘不了。
- Liǎo 了 (pay attention to the pronunciation) is used after a verb as a complement to 得 or 不 to indicate possibility.

148. I'll walk you to the door.
Wǒ sòng nǐ dào ménkǒu 我送你到门口。

🎧 149. Give my regards to him.
Nǐ dài wǒ xiàng tā wènhǎo 你代我向他问好。

150. Please say hello to your family.
Qǐng dài wǒ xiàng nǐde jiārén wènhǎo
请代我向你的家人问好。

🎧 151. Give me a call sometime.
Yǒu kòng gěi wǒ dǎ diànhuà 有空给我打电话。
- Dǎ 打 is one of the most common verbs in Chinese with many different meanings: strike, fight, construct, make. In dǎ diànhuà 打电话, dǎ 打 means send or dispatch, and dǎ diànhuà 打电话 means make a phone call.

152. Please ask him to give me a call.
Qǐng tā dǎ ge diànhuà gěi wǒ 请他打个电话给我。

153. Let's get together sometime.
Yǒu shíjiān wǒmen zài jù yíxià ba
有时间我们再聚一下吧。

154. I hope to see you again soon.
Xīwàng bùjiǔ néng zài jiàndào nǐ
希望不久能再见到你。

155. See you again in the near future.
Hòu huì yǒu qí 后会有期。

 Conversation Starters

156. I heard….
Tīng shuō 听说。

- This is used when you want to bring up a subject you heard from someone else or somewhere else.

157. You listen to me.
Nǐ tīng wǒ shuō 你听我说。

158. I want to ask about……:
Dǎting yíxià 打听一下。

MORE: Listen
Hear or listen :tīng 听
Talk or speak. shuō 说
Read : dú 读
Write : xiě 写

🔊159. It's a fine day。
Jīntiān shì ge hǎo tiān 今天是个好天。
- Gè 个 is the most extensively used measure word, especially before nouns which do not have special measure words of their own.

160. What a nice day it is!
Jīntiān tiānqì zhēn hǎo 今天天气真好!

161. A lovely day, isn't it?
Tiānqì hěn hǎo, shì ba 天气很好，是吧?
- Ba 吧 is used at the end of the sentence to indicate agreement or approval.

🔊162. What's the weather today?
Jīntiān tiānqì zěnme yàng 今天天气怎么样?

> **MORE: Days**
> Yesterday zuótiān 昨天
> Today :jīntiān 今天
> Tomorrow: míngtiān 明天
> 3 days earlier: sān tiān zhī qián 3天之前
> 5 days later: wǔ tiān zhī hòu 5天之后

163. It's fine.
Tiānqì zhēn hǎo 天气很好。

164. What horrible weather!
Zhè guǐ tiānqì 这鬼天气!

165. Weather is not nice today.
Jīntiān tiānqì bù hǎo 今天天气不好。

🔊166. It is growing cool。
Tiānqì jiànjiàn liángshuǎng qǐlai 天气渐渐凉爽起来。

167. It's cold today.
Jīntiān tiānqì hěn lěng 今天天气很冷。

168. It's getting cold.
Tiānqì lěng qǐlai le 天气冷起来了。
- Qǐlai 起来 indicates the beginning and the continuation of an action.

169. Today is colder than yesterday.
Jīntiān bǐ zuótiān lěng 今天比昨天冷。

170. It's going to rain.
Yào xià yǔ le 要下雨了。

171. Spring is the best season here.
Chūntiān shì zhèli zuì hǎode jìjié
春天是这里最好的季节。

	MORE: Seasons
	Summer: xiàtiān 夏天
	Fall: qiūtiān 秋天
	Winter: dōngtiān 冬天

172. Guess what?
Cāi cāi kàn 猜猜看?

173. Let me guess.
Ràng wǒ cāi yi cāi 让我猜一猜。

174. I can't guess it right.
Wǒ cāi bù zháo 我猜不着。
- Zháo 着 is used after a verb to indicate result.

175. What's up?
Yǒu shénme shì ma 有什么事吗?

🎧 176. What's new?
Yǒu shénme xīnxiān shì ma
有什么新鲜事吗?

177. How are things going?
Shìqing jìnzhǎnde zěnyàng 事情进展得怎样?

🎧 178. What happened to you?
Nǐ zěnme le 你怎么了?

🎧 179. What's wrong with you?
Nǐ nǎli bú duìjìnr 你哪里不对劲儿?
- Drop the "n" sound in duìjìnr 对劲儿.

180. It drives me crazy.
Tā shǐ wǒ kuài yào fāfēng le 它使我快要发疯了。
- Yào 要 as a verb has many meanings. When yào 要 is used with le 了, it means to be going to, such as in we are going to play.

MORE: He, She and It
He: tā 他
She: tā 她 (If you look at the left side of the characters, the radical of 他 is 亻, which is from the letter 人 meaning people.
Radical of 她 is 女, which indicates many female things.)
When gender is not necessary or possible, usually "tā 他"is used.
It: tā 它 Neuter gender
He, she, and it are all the same pronunciation tā, and they are only recognizable when written.
They in English can be 3 kinds in Chinese:
Tā 他 (he) + men 们 ("s"-plural numbers) = tāmen 他们 (they)
Tā 她 (she) + men 们 ("s"-plural numbers) = tāmen 她们 (they)
Tā 它 (it) + men 们 ("s"-plural numbers) = tāmen 它们 (they)

🎧 181. It's a long story.
Shuō lái huà cháng 说来话长。

🎧182. You look great.
Nǐ kàn shàngqu búcuò 你看上去不错。
- Shàngqu 上去 is used after a verb to indicate a distance farther away from the speaker.

183. You look good too.
Nǐ yě yíyàng 你也一样。

🎧184. You haven't changed much.
Nǐ méi zěnme biàn 你没怎么变。

185. Neither have you.
Nǐ yě méi biàn 你也没变。

186. You've really changed.
Nǐ biàn yàng le 你变样了。

🎧187. You've grown up
Nǐ zhǎng dà le 你长大了。

188. Look how much you've grown up.
Kàn nǐ dōu zhǎng zhème dà le 看你都长这么大了!

🎧189. You've become so beautiful.
Nǐ yuè lái yuè piàoliang le 你越来越漂亮了。

190. Are you gaining weight lately?
Zuìjìn nǐ shì búshì pàng le 最近你是不是胖了?

191. I'm afraid so.
Hǎoxiàng shì ba 好像是吧。

🎧192. Are you losing weight?
Nǐ shì búshì shòu le 你是不是瘦了?

MORE: Asking Questions in Chinese
There are 3 ways of making question sentences in Chinese.
  1. Using interrogative pronouns, such as what, why, who, how.
What's your name?: Nǐ jiào shénme míngzi 你叫什么名字?
2. Using ma 吗, an interrogative particle used at the end of the declarative sentence.
  Are you healthy?: Nǐ shēntǐ hǎo ma? 你身体好吗?
3. Alternate possibilities between an affirmative and negative predicate.
  Is that right? Shì búshì 是不是? = shì 是(affirmative) + búshì 不是 (negative)

193. Your hair looks very stylish.
Nǐde fàxíng hěn shímáo 你的发型很时髦。

194. I got a haircut yesterday.
Wǒ shì zuótiān lǐde fà 我是昨天理的发。

195. Do you like swimming?
Nǐ xǐhuan yóuyǒng ma 你喜欢游泳吗?

196. Do you like travel?
Nǐ xǐhuan lǚxíng ma 你喜欢旅行吗?

 MORE: Lǚ 旅
Lǚ 旅 itself means travel, and is used in many terms related to travel. For example:
Lǚkè 旅客: guest, passenger (airplane or train broadcast usually starts with gèwèi lǚkè 各位旅客 means dear passengers)
Lǚxíng 旅行 : general term for travel (xíng 行 -go)
Lǚxíng shè 旅行社 : travel agency (shè 社-company)

197. Do you like movies?
Nǐ xǐhuan kàn diànyǐng ma 你喜欢看电影吗?

198. What kind of movies do you like?

Nǐ xǐhuan nǎ yí lèi de diànyǐng 你喜欢哪一类的电影?

199. I like artistic films.
Wǒ xǐhuan kàn wényì piān 我喜欢看文艺片。

 MORE: Movies
Action films: dòngzuò piān 动作片
Romantic films:: àiqíng piān 愛情片
Horror films: kǒngbù piān 恐怖片

200. Do you like ice-cream?
Nǐ xǐ bu xǐhuan chī bīngqílín
你喜不喜欢吃冰淇淋?

201. I'm a night person.
Wǒ shì ge yè māozi 我是个夜猫子。
   • This literally means a night cat!!

202. I'm not.
Wǒ kě búshì 我可不是。
   • Kě 可 is used to emphasize the tone of the speaker.

203. I'm a morning person.
Wǒ xǐhuan zǎo qǐ 我喜欢早起。

204. Coffee gets me going.
Wǒ shì yòng kāfēi lái tíshén de
我是用咖啡来提神的。

 MORE: Coffee
Espresso: tè nóng kāfēi 特浓咖啡
Cappuccino: nǎi mò kāfēi 奶沫咖啡
Café Latte: xiāng nǎi kāfēi 香奶咖啡
Black Coffee: hēi kāfēi 黑咖啡

Asking What, Who, Where, and How

205. What is this?
Zhè shì shénme 这是什么？

206. What are those?
Nà xiē shì shénme 那些是什么？

 MORE: This and That
Zhè 这 is a pronoun meaning this. The opposite word of zhè 这 is nà 那, means that.
Zhè 这 (this) ↔ Nà 那 (that)
Zhèr 这儿 (here) ↔ Nàr 那儿 (there) (ér 儿 makes retroflex ending after nouns)
Zhè xiē 这些 (these) ↔ Nà xiē 那些 (those) (xiē 些 is a measuring word, means some)

---

207. What's going on?
Fāshēng shénme shì le 发生什么事了？

208. What should I do?
Wǒ gāi zěnme bàn 我该怎么办？

209. Just do it this way.
Jiù zhème bàn 就这么办。

210. What are you doing?
Nǐ gànmá ne 你干吗呢？

211. What's up?
Yǒu shénme shì ma 有什么事吗？

🎧212. What do you think?

Nǐ zěnme rènwei 你怎么认为？

213. What is taking so long?

Zěnme huā nàme cháng shíjiān 怎么花那么长时间？
- Huā 花 means flower as a noun, but when it is used as a verb it means spend.

🎧214. What's on your mind?

Nǐ xiǎng shénme ne 你想什么呢？

215. Nothing.

Méi (xiǎng) shénme 没(想)什么。

🎧216. What are you looking for?

Nǐ zhǎo shénme dōngxi 你找什么东西？
- Dōng 东 means east and xī 西 means west, but together as dōngxi 东西 it means a thing (xi 西 is a neutral tone). When you say cardinal East-West, it is dōng xī 东西, xī 西 as a first tone.

🎧217. What are you talking about?

Nǐ shuō shénme 你说什么？

218. What are you trying to say?

Nǐ yào shuō shénme 你要说什么？
- Because of yào 要, this question includes the intention or will.

219. What is he talking about?

Tā zài shuō xiē shénme
他在说些什么？

220. What kind of music do you like?

Nǐ xǐhuan tīng shénme yīnyuè 你喜欢听什么音乐？

221. What are your plans for the weekend?
Nǐ zhōumò jìhuà zuò shénme 你周末计划做什么？

222. Why?
Wèi shénme 为什么？

223. Why?
Gànmá 干嘛？
- Gànmá 干嘛 is colloquial and more informal than wèi shénme 为什么.

224. Who is it?
Shéi ya 谁呀？

225. Guess who I bumped into yesterday?
Nǐ cāi wǒ zuótiān yùjiàn shéi le 你猜我昨天遇见谁了？

226. Who is he/she?
Tā shì shéi 他/她是谁？

227. Who told you that?
Shéi gàosu nì de 谁告诉你的？

228. Which one do you want?
Nì yào nǎ yí ge 你要哪一个？

229. Where were we?
Wǒmen shuōdào nǎr le 我们说到哪儿了？

230. Where is he?
Tā zài nǎli 他在哪里？

231. Where are you going?
Nǐ qù nǎr 你去哪儿？

MORE: qù 去 and zǒu 走

Zǒu 走 and qù 去 both mean go or leave. Usually zǒu 走 is used to go from a place and qù 去 is used to go to a destination. Compare the below sentences.

When are you leaving?
(O) Nǐ shénme shíhou zǒu 你什么时候走?
(O) Nǐ shénme shíhou qù 你什么时候去?
Where are you going?
(O) Nǐ qù nǎr 你去哪儿?
(X) Nǐ zǒu nǎr 你走哪儿? (This sentence is wrong.)

232. Where do you want to go?
Nǐ yào qù nǎr 你要去哪儿?

- Because of yào 要, this question includes the intention or will.

233. Where have you been?
Nǐ qù nǎr le 你去哪儿了?

- Le 了 - a particle indicating change.

234. How did he do?
Tā zuòde zěnme yàng 他做得怎么样?

235. He did a good job.
Tā zuòde hěn hǎo 他做得很好。

236. How's he getting along these days?
Tā zhè xiē rìzi guòde zěnme yàng
他这些日子过得怎么样?

237. How long did it last?
Chíxùle duōjiù 持续了多久?

238. How can I get in touch with you?
Wǒ zěnyàng gēn nǐ liánluò shàng

我怎样能跟你联络上？

- Shàng 上 is used after a verb to indicate the beginning and the continuity of an action.

239. When are you leaving?

Nǐ shénme shíhou zǒu 你什么时候走？

- Shíjiān 时间 and shíhou 时候 both mean time, including the duration of time. But shíjiān 时间 means a concept of time as well. For example, time and space is shíjiān yǔ kōngjiān 时间与空间.

Numbers, Times and Dates

240.

Zero: líng 零
One : yī 一
Two : èr 二
Three : sān 三
Four : sì 四
Five : wǔ 五
Six : liù 六
Seven : qī 七
Eight : bā 八
Nine : jiǔ 九
Ten : shí 十
Hundred: bǎi 百
Thousand: qiān 千

241. What's the temperature today?

Jīntiān qìwēn duōshao 今天气温多少？

- Shǎo 少 (originally a 3rd tone) shouldn't be confused with xiǎo

小. Shǎo 少 has a left-falling stroke, called piě 撇 at the bottom. xiǎo 小 (small) & shǎo 少 (few, little)
- In China, celsius is used for temperature. Along with qìwēn 气温, wēndù 温度 is also a common term for temperature (dù 度 means degree).
  Celsius: shè shì 摄氏
  Fahrenheit : huá shì 华氏

242. It's 23 degree today.
Jīntiān èr shí sān dù 今天 二十三度。

MORE: Numbers		
11 : shí yī 十一	12 : shí èr 十二	13 : shí sān 十三
14 : shí sì 十四	15 : shí wǔ 十五	16 : shí liù 十六
17 : shí qī 十七	18 : shí bā 十八	19 : shí jiǔ 十九
20 : èr shí 二十	30 : sān shí 三十	40 : sì shí 四十

243. It's minus 15 degree today, very cold.
Jīntiān língxià shí wǔ dù, hěn lěng
今天零下十五度，很冷。

244. What time is it?
Jǐ diǎn le 几点了？

245. Excuse me, what time it is now?
Qǐngwèn, xiànzài jǐ diǎn 请问，现在几点？

246. About what time?
Dàyuē jǐ diǎn 大约几点？

247. It's 5 o'clock.
Wǔ diǎn le 五点了。

248. It's ten to two.
Chā shí fēn liǎng diǎn 差十分两点。

- We learned number two as èr 二, and here is another term for two, liǎng 两. Grammatically there are different ways of using them, such as èr 二 is an ordinal number and liǎng 两 is used with a measure word.

MORE: èr 二 and liǎng 两
2: èr 二, liǎng 两
20: èr shí 二十
200: èr bái 二百, liǎng bái 两百

249. It's a quarter to nine.
Xiànzaì chā yíkè jiǔ diǎn 现在差一刻九点。

250. It's 8:15.
Bā diǎn yí kè 八点一刻。

251. It's 7: 36
Qī diǎn sān shí liù fēn 七点三十六分。

252. It's half past nine.
Xiànzaì jiǔ diǎn bàn 现在 9 点半。

253. The clock is five minutes slow (fast).
Nà zhī biǎo màn (kuài) wǔ fēn zhōng
那只表慢(快)5 分钟。

254. I killed two hours watching TV.
Wǒ kànle liǎng ge xiǎoshíde diànshì yǐ dǎfā shíjiān
我看了两个小时的电视以打发时间。

- Yǐ 以 means in order to, which is a preposition indicating purpose.

255. I am late by an hour.
Wǒ wǎn le yí ge xiǎoshí 我晚了一个小时。

256. I ran for a half hour.
Wǒ pǎole bàn ge xiǎoshí 我跑了半个小时。

257. He slept for 11 hours.
Tā shuìle shí yí ge zhōngtóu 他睡了十一个钟头.

258. Do you have some free time?
Nǐ yǒu kōngxiánde shíjiān ma 你有空闲的时间吗?

259. What day is today?
Jīntiān (shì) xīngqī jǐ 今天(是)星期几?

260. It's Sunday today.
Jīntiān shì xīngqī tiān 今天是星期天。

MORE: Days of the Week	
Monday: xīngqī yī	星期一
Tuesday: xīngqī èr	星期二
Wednesday: xīngqī sān	星期三
Thursday: xīngqī sì	星期四
Friday: xīngqī wǔ	星期五
Saturday: xīngqī liù	星期六
Sunday: xīngqī tiān	星期天
Last week : shàng xīngqī	上星期
This week : zhè xīngqī	这星期
Next week: xià xīngqī	下星期

261. Today is August 2nd.
Jīntiān bā yuè èr hào 今天八月二号。

262. What month is it?
Jīntiān jǐ yuè fèn 今天几月份?

263. It's May.
Wǔ yuè 五月。

MORE: Month

January: yī yuè 一月

February: èr yuè 二月

March: sān yuè 三月

April: sì yuè 四月

May: wǔ yuè 五月

June: liù yuè 六月

July: qī yuè 七月

August: bā yuè 八月

September: jiǔ yuè 九月

October: shí yuè 十月

November: shí yī yuè 十一月

December: shí èr yuè 十二月

264. What's today's date?
Jīntiān jǐ hào 今天几号?

MORE: Dates

1st : yī hào 一号

2nd : èr hào 二号

3rd : sān hào 三号

5th : wǔ hào 五号

10th : shí hào 十号

13th : shí sān hào 十三号

14th : shí sì hào 十四号

17th : shí qī hào 十七号

20th : èr shí hào 二十号

26th : èr shí liù hào 二十六号

28th : èr shí bā hào 二十八号

30th : sān shí hào 三十号

31st : sān shí yī hào 三十一号

265. When is your birthday?
Nǐde shēngrì shì jǐ yuè jǐ hào
你的生日是几月几号?

266. My birthday is March 16th.
Wǒde shēngrì shì sān yuè shí liù hào
我的生日是三月十六号。

267. I'll come again in a couple of days.
Wǒ guò liǎng tiān zài lái 我过两天再来。

> **MORE: Days**
> If you are doing business with Chinese, you probably hear guò liǎng tiān 过两天 or zhè liǎng tiān 这两天 terms a lot, when you ask for exact dates. These two sound similar but what they mean are quite different.
> Guò liǎng tiān 过两天: in a couple of days (could be up to 10 days)
> Zhè liǎng tiān 这两天: these two days, means today or tomorrow (could be up to 5 days)
> Guò jǐ tiān 过几天: in a few days (could be up to a month)

268. Five more days to go.
Zài děng wǔ tiān ba 再等五天吧。

269. Only three days left.
Zhǐ shèngxia sān tiān le 只剩下三天了。
- Xia 下 is used after a verb as a complement indicating the completion or result of an action.

270. I wasted a whole day.
Báibái làngfèile yì zhěng tiān 白白浪费了一整天。

 Making an Appointment

271. Are you free this weekend?
Zhè ge zhōumò nǐ yǒukòng ma
这个周末你有空吗？

272. Um, I am.
Ng, yǒukòng 嗯，有空。
- Ng 嗯 is an interjection indicating response.

273. No, I have plans.
Bù, wǒ yǒu ānpái 不，我有安排。

🎧274. I'm free on Friday.
Xīngqī wǔ yǒukòng 星期五有空。

🎧275. Do you have any plans this afternoon?
Nǐ jīntiān xiàwǔ yǒu ānpái ma
你今天下午有安排吗?

276. No, nothing special.
Méiyǒu, méiyǒu shéme tèbiéde ānpái
没有，没有什么特别的安排。

🎧277. Um, I need to work.
Ng, wǒ děi gōngzuò 嗯，我得工作。

278. Are you busy this afternoon?
Jīntiān xiàwǔ nǐ máng ma 今天下午你忙吗?

🎧279. How about having a dinner together?
Yìqǐ chī wǎnfàn zénme yàng
一起吃晚饭怎么样?

🎧280. Sounds great!
Nà tài hǎo le 那太好了!

🎧281. Let's have a drink.
Qù hē yì bēi ba 去喝一杯吧。

🎧282. When can I come over?
Wǒ shénme shíhou qù héshì 我什么时候去合适?

283. When can I visit?

Wǒ shénme shíhou néng qù bàifǎng nín

我什么时候能去拜访您?

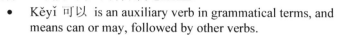

284. When can I stop by your place?

Wǒ shénme shíhou kěyǐ qù nǐ nàr zuò zuò

我什么时候可以去你那儿坐坐?

- Kěyǐ 可以 is an auxiliary verb in grammatical terms, and means can or may, followed by other verbs.

285. When is it convenient for you?

Nǐ shénme shíhou fāngbiàn 你什么时候方便?

286. It's hard to say.

Hěn nán shuō 很难说。

287. Is seven convenient for you?

Qī diǎn fāngbiàn ma 7 点你方便吗?

288. When will it be ready?

Shénme shíhou néng zhǔnbèi hǎo 什么时候能准备好?

289. I'm pressed for time.

Wǒ gǎn shíjiān 我赶时间。

290. Is it too early (late)?

Tài zǎo (wǎn) le ma 太早(晚)了吗?

291. Catch me later.

Guò huìr zài lái zhǎo wǒ 过会儿再来找我。

292. That's a bad day for me.

Nà tiān wǒ bù xíng 那天我不行。

293. Maybe some other time.
Yěyǔ xià yí cì ba 也许下一次吧。

294. Can we do it some other time?
Lìng zhǎo shíjiān kěyǐ ma
另找时间可以吗?

295. I am so sorry, I have plans.
Zhēn duìbuqǐ, wǒ lìng yǒu ānpái
真对不起,我另有安排。

296. I am so sorry, I am afraid not.
Shízài duìbuqǐ, kǒngpà bù xíng
实在对不起,恐怕不行。

297. Thank you for your invitation, but…..
Xièxiè nínde yāoqǐng, kěshì 谢谢您的邀请,可是……

298. Whenever.
Shénme shíhou dōu xíng 什么时候都行。

299. Whenever you are free.
Shénme shíhou dōu xíng, zhǐyào nǐ yǒu shíjiān
什么时候都行,只要你有时间。

300. Any day will do.
Nǎ yì tiān dōu xíng 哪一天都行。

301. That day is fine
Nà tiān wǒ kěyǐ 那天我可以。

- If this letter nà 那 looks familiar to you, you are right! It looks like the interrogative pronoun nǎ 哪 (means which), but nǎ 哪 has 口 on the left side. nà 那 (that) ↔ nǎ 哪 (which).

302. Any day of the week is fine.
Xīngqī jǐ dōu xíng 星期几都行。

303. I'm free all day.
Wǒ yì zhěngtiān dōu yǒukòng 我一整天都有空。

304. I'll leave it up to you.
Quán jiāo gěi nǐ le 全交给你了。

305. It's your decision.
Nǐ dìng ba 你定吧。

306. Okay, see you then.
Xíng, dào shíhou jiàn 行，到时候见。

307. I'll see you at six.
Wǒ liù diǎnzhong jiàn nǐ 我六点钟见你。

Expressing Thoughts and Feelings

308. Yes
Shì 是。

- Shì 是 is a verb meaning to be, but it is also used to answer in the affirmative, meaning "yes" or "right" to questions.

309. No
Búshì 不是。

310. Is that right?
Duì bú duì 对不对？

🎧311. Sure. Go ahead.
Dāngrán, qǐngbiàn 当然, 请便。

312. Me too.
Wǒ yě shì 我也是。

313. Same here.
Wǒ yě yíyàng 我也一样。

🎧314. I think so.
Wǒ rènwei shì zhèyàng de 我认为是这样的。

315. I think so too.
Wǒ yě zhème xiǎng 我也这么想。

🎧316. Let me think.
Ràng wǒ xiǎng yi xiǎng 让我想一想。

- Yī 一 means one, but when it's used between the same verbs it is indicating that the action occurs once or for a short period of time.

🎧317. I'll think it over.
Wǒ zǐxì kǎolǜ yíxià 我仔细考虑一下。

- We have learned that bù 不 becomes 2nd tone before a 4th tone. Besides bù 不, there are 3 more characters having the same tone changes. They are yī 一 (one), qī 七 (seven) and bā 八 (eight), which are called "yīqībābù 一七八不" tone change. This is one of the few important tone changes to memorize. Yī 一 is originally a first tone. However, it will be pronounced as a second tone when it is followed by a fourth tone, as it is in yíxià 一下.

318. Do you understand?
Nǐ míngbai ma 你明白吗?

🎧319. I understand.
Wǒ míngbai 我明白。

320. I don't understand.
Wǒ bù míngbai 我不明白。

321. I don't understand very well.
Wǒ bú tài míngbai 我不太明白。

🎧322. Why don't you understand?
Nǐ zěnme bù míngbai 你怎么不明白?

323. Do you see it? (Do you understand now?)
Nǐ míngbai le ma 你明白了吗?

324. I see. (Now I understand.)
Wǒ míngbai le 我明白了。
- Le 了 - a particle indicating change.

🎧325. I don't understand what you are talking about.
Wǒ bù míngbai nǐ shuō shénme 我不明白你说什么。

326. Have you got that?
Nǐ míngbai wǒde yìsi ma 你明白我的意思吗?

327. I don't know.
Wǒ bù zhīdào 我不知道。

🎧328. No one knows.
Méiyǒu rén zhīdào 没有人知道。

329. I knew it.
Wǒ zǎo zhīdào le 我早知道了。

🎧 330. That's good to know.

Xìnghǎo zhīdàole zhè jiàn shì 幸好知道了这件事。

🎧 331. I have no idea.

Wǒ yìdiǎnr dōu bù zhīdào 我一点儿都不知道。

- This literally means I don't know even a little. Yīdiǎnr 一点儿 is usually used in positive sentences, and is used with dōu 都 or yě 也 in negative sentences. In the word yìdiǎnr 一点儿, diǎn 点 is used as a measure word meaning a little, so yìdiǎnr 一点儿 doesn't mean one o'clock!! One o'clock is yī diǎn 一点 without the ér 儿.

🎧 332. I have no clue.

Wǒ méiyǒu tóuxù 我没有头绪。

333. I wasn't aware of that.

Wǒ méiyǒu yìshì dào 我没有意识到。

334. I noticed that.

Wǒ zhùyìdào le 我注意到了。

🎧 335. I agree.

Wǒ tóngyì 我同意。

336. I don't agree.

Wǒ bù tóngyì 我不同意。

🎧 337. Why not?

Wèi shénme bù ne 为什么不呢?

🎧 338. Not bad.

Hái búcuò 还不错。

339. Cool!

Hěn kù 很酷！
- The word kù 酷 is the transliteration of the word English cool.

340. Just wonderful!
Jiǎnzhí tài bàng le 简直太棒了!

341. It sounds great!
Tīng qǐlai hěn búcuò 听起来很不错。
- Qǐlai 起来 means get up or stand up. It also comes after a verb indicating upward movement, the beginning and the continuation of an action, the completion of an action, or fulfillment of a purpose.

342. That's a good idea.
Zhè ge zhǔyì zhēn búcuò 这个主意真不错。

343. I have a good idea!
Wǒ yǒu yí ge hǎo zhǔyì 我有一个好主意。

344. That's a terrific idea!
Zhēn shì hǎo zhǔyì 真是好主意!

345. That makes sense.
Nà kěyǐ lǐjiě 那可以理解。

346. What he said makes sense.
Tā shuōde huà hěn yǒu dàoli 他说的话很有道理。

347. I don't blame you. (I understand how you feel.)
Wǒ lǐjiě nǐde xīnqíng 我理解你的心情。

348. You can say that again!
Pō yǒu tónggǎn 颇有同感。

349. You will have to wait and see.

Nǐ děi děng yi děng kàn 你得等一等看。

350. Do you mean it?
Nǐ shì dāng zhēnde ma 你是当真的吗？

351. Is it serious?
Yánzhòng ma 严重吗？

352. Forget it.
Suàn le 算了!

353. Give me a break.
Bié suíbiàn xiā shuō 别随便瞎说。

354. I promise.
Wǒ bǎozhèng 我保证。

355. I decline.
Wǒ jùjué 我拒绝。

356. I doubt it.
Wǒ huáiyí 我怀疑。

357. There is no doubt about it.
Nà shì háo wú yíwèn de 那是毫无疑问的。

358. It's up to you.
Yóu nǐ juédìng 由你决定。

359. That depends.
Nà děi kàn qíngkuàng 那得看情况。

360. It all depends.

Shì qíngxing ér dìng 视情形而定。

🎧361. Trust me.
Xiāngxìn wǒ 相信我。

🎧362. Take my word for it.
Xiāngxìn wǒde huà 相信我的话。

363. I'll pay attention.
Wǒ huì liúyì de 我会留意的。

🎧364. Don't worry. I'll take care of it.
Fàngxīn, bāo zài wǒ shēnshang 放心，包在我身上。
- Shang 上 is used after nouns to indicate the surface of an object.

365. It's out of the question.
Zhè shì bù kěnéng de 这是不可能的。

🎧366. There's a possibility.
Yǒu zhè ge kěnéng 有这个可能。

367. I couldn't help it.
Wǒ méiyǒu bànfǎ 我没有办法。

🎧368. There is nothing I can do.
Wǒ wú néng wéi lì 我无能为力。

369. I wish I could.
Dàn yuàn wǒ néng 但愿我能。

370. I have no choice.
Wǒ bié wú xuǎnzé 我别无选择。

371. You're always right.
Nǐ zǒngshì duì de 你总是对的。

372. Everyone has a different point of view.
Měi ge rénde kànfǎ dōu bù yíyàng
每个人的看法都不一样。

373. You are thinking too much.
Nǐ xiǎng tài duō le 你想太多了。

374. Don't give free rein to fancy.
Búyào húsī luànxiǎng 不要胡斯乱想。

375. Let's get to the point.
Ràng wǒmen yán guī zhèng zhuàn
让我们言归正传。

376. Is there any problem?
Yǒu wèntí ma 有问题吗?
   • This also means "do you have any questions?" based on the situation.

377. There is a problem.
Yǒu wèntí 有问题。
   • Usually this implies that things may not work out.

378. There is a little problem.
Yǒu diǎn wèntí 有点问题。
   • Usually this implies that there is a little problem, but things will most likely work out.

379. Is it a big problem?
Wèntí dà bú dà 问题大不大?

380. We can work it out.

Wǒmen kěyǐ jiějué zhè ge wèntí
我们可以解决这个问题。

🎧381. Something must be done about it.
Bìxū děi xiǎng ge bànfǎ 必须得想个办法。

382. Maybe it will work.
Yěxǔ zhè ge bànfǎ huì yǒuxiào 也许这个办法会有效。
- Huì 会 means to be likely to.

🎧383. I don't remember it.
Wǒ jì bu qīngchu le 我记不清楚了。

384. I think……
Wǒ xiǎng 我想…….。

🎧385. I remember it now.
Wǒ xiǎng qǐlai le 我想起来了。

386. I don't remember it.
Wǒ xiǎng bù qǐlai 我想不起来。

387. It will come to me.
Wǒ huì xiǎng qǐlai de 我会想起来的。

388. That rings a bell.
Wǒ zǒngsuàn xiǎng qǐlai le 我总算想起来了。
- Qǐlai 起来 indicates completion of an action.

🎧389. I have an impression.
Wǒ yǒu yìnxiàng 我有印象。

🎧390. It doesn't matter to me.
Zhè duì wǒ lái shuō wúsuǒwèi 这对我来说无所谓。

391. Please let me know.
Qǐng gàosu wǒ yì shēng 请告诉我一声。

🎧392. I can't wait any longer.
Wǒ bù néng zài děng le 我不能再等了。

393. What a coincidence!
Zhēn shì tài qiǎo le 真是太巧了!

394. That's the way it is.
Jiùshì zhème huí shì 就是这么回事。

🎧395. This is the way it should be.
Zhè shì lǐ suǒ dāngrán de shì 这是理所当然的事。

396. Count me on.
Suànshàng wǒ 算上我。

397. I can't follow you.
Wǒ bù dǒng nǐ shuō de 我不懂你说的。

🎧398. This is just what I need.
Zhè zhèng shì wǒ suǒ xūyào de 这正是我所需要的。

🎧399. I am so happy (sad).
Wǒ hěn gāoxìng (shāngxīn) 我很高兴(伤心)。

400. I am afraid of snakes.
Wǒ pà shé 我怕蛇。

🎧401. That gives me goose bumps.
Tā shǐ wǒ qǐ jīpí gēda 它使我起鸡皮疙瘩。

402. I was touched.

Wǒ hěn shòu gǎndòng 我很受感动。

🎧403. I feel so lonely.
Wǒ gǎndào fēicháng jìmò 我感到非常寂寞。

> **MORE: Good and Very good**
> Good: hǎo 好
> Not bad: búcuò 不错 (cuò 错- bad, wrong)
> Very good: tǐng hǎo 挺好 (tǐng 挺- very, quite)
> Really good : zhēn hǎo 真好 (zhēn 真 - really)
> Better : gèng hǎo 更好 (gèng 更 - more, further)
> Best : zuì hǎo 最好 (zuì 最 - most)
> Extremely good: fēicháng hǎo 非常好 (fēicháng 非常-extremely)
> If you compare the strength of these adverbs, fēicháng 非常 should be
> the strongest.
> Hěn hǎo 很好< gèng hǎo 更好< zuì hǎo 最好< fēicháng hǎo 非常好

🎧404. It's too bad !
Zhēn zāogāo 真糟糕！

🎧405. What a pity!
Tài yíhàn le 太遗憾了!

406. What a shame!
Zhēn shì yíhàn 真是遗憾!

407. It rather surprised me.
Nà jiàn shì shǐ wǒ pō gǎn jīngyà 那件事使我颇感惊讶。

🎧408. I'm looking forward to it.
Wǒ pānwàngzhe zhè jiàn shì 我盼望着这件事。
   • Zhe 着 indicates an action in progress.

409. I didn't even dream about it.
Wǒ zuòmèng yě xiǎngbudào 我做梦也想不到。

🔊410. I'm glad to hear that.
Tīngdào zhè xiāoxi wǒ hěn gāoxìng
听到这消息我很高兴。

411. I could hardly speak.
Wǒ jiǎnzhí shuō bu chū huà lái 我简直说不出话来。
- Chūlái 出来 is used after a verb to indicate outward movement.

🔊412. I feel no regret for it.
Duì zhè jiàn shì wǒ bù juéde hòuhuǐ
对这件事我不觉得后悔。

413. This is my first time and last time.
Zhè shì wǒde dì yícì yě shì zuì hòu yícì
这是我的第一次也是最后一次。

 **Encouragements**

🔊414. Good job!
Zuòde hǎo 做得好!
- Zuò 做 is a general term for do, make, or be. Dé 得 is a particle used between a verb or an adjective and its complement to indicate result, possibility, or degree. Hǎo 好 means good or well, and it complements the verb zuò 做 indicating the degree.

🔊415. Let's make things better!
Ràng wǒmen zuòde gèng hǎo 让我们做得更好!

416. Do it right!
Bǎ tā zuò duì 把它做对。

- Object comes after a verb in Chinese. But this is an exception. Bǎ 把 is a preposition bringing an object before the verb, which implies the strong "placement" meaning.

417. You did it right.
Nǐ zuòde duì 你做得对。

🎧418. You can make it!
Nǐ néng zuòdào 你能做到!
- Dào 到 is used after a verb as a complement to indicate success.

419. I just made it!
Wǒ zuòdào le 我做到了!

420. I bet you can.
Wǒ quèxìn nǐ néng zuòdào 我确信你能做到。

🎧421. You did fairly well!
Nǐ gànde xiāngdāng búcuò 你干得相当不错。

422. I'm very proud of you.
Wǒ wèi nǐ gǎndào fēicháng jiāoào
我为你感到非常骄傲。

🎧423. Do as you please.
Nǐ yào zěnme bàn jiù zěnme bàn
你要怎么办就怎么办。
- Zěnme 怎么 indicates the nature, condition, or manner in general.

424. I'm worried about you.
Wǒ yǒudiǎn dānxīn nǐ 我有点担心你。

425. I will be more careful.

Wǒ huì xiǎoxīn yìxiē de 我会小心一些的。

426. I will never forget it.
Wǒ huì jìzhe de 我会记着的。

🎧427. If I were you, I would do the same thing.
Huànle shì wǒ, yě huì zhème zuò
换了是我, 也会这么做。

428. I'm on your side.
Wǒ quánlì zhīchí nǐ 我全力支持你。

🎧429. Cheers!!!
Jiāyóu jiāyóu 加油加油!!

430. Keep it up!
Jiānchí xiàqù 坚持下去!
  - Xiàqù下去 is used to indicate the continuation of an action.

🎧431. Give it a try.
Shì yi shì 试一试。
  - Yī 一 means one, and can be used between the same verbs indicating that the action occurs once or lasts for a short time.

432. Try again.
Zài shì shì 再试试。

433. Hang in there.
Jiāyóu ba 加油吧!
  - Ba 吧 is used a the end of the sentence to indicate suggestion, request, or command.

🎧434. Don't worry.
Bié dānxīn 别担心。

🎧435. Cheer up!
Zhēnzuò qǐlái 振作起来!

436. Pull yourself together.
Dǎ qǐ jīngshén lái 打起精神来。

🎧437. Do you feel better?
Hǎo diǎn le ma 好点了吗?

🎧438. Smile!!!
Xiào yi xiào 笑一笑!!!

439. Take it easy.
Bié jǐnzhāng 别紧张。

440. I'll do my best.
Wǒ jiāng huì jìn wǒ zuì dà nǔlì 我将会尽我最大努力。
  • Jiāng 将 is a adverb meaning to be going to.

🎧441. I'll try my best.
Wǒ jìn lì ér wéi 我尽力而为。

442. Do your best!
Jìn nǐde quánlì 尽你的全力!

🎧443. Don't try your luck!
Búyào pèng yùnqì 不要碰运气。

🎧444. Don't panic.
Búbì jīnghuāng 不必惊慌。

445. Don't lose your head.
Búyào jīnghuāng shīcuò 不要惊慌失措。

446. Can you give me some feedback?
Nǐ néng gěi wǒ yì xiē jiànyì ma 你能给我一些建议吗？

447. Thanks for the encouragement.
Xièxiè nǐde gǔlì 谢谢你的鼓励!

448. Let's hope for the best.
Wǒmen wǎng hǎochù xiǎng ba 我们往好处想吧。

449. Things will be better tomorrow.
Míngtiān huì gèng hǎo 明天会更好。

450. You should take advantage of it.
Nǐ yīnggāi hǎohǎo lìyòng zhè ge jīhuì
你应该好好利用这个机会。

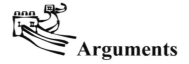 **Arguments**

451. I quit!
Wǒ búgàn le 我不干了!

452. Let go!
Fàngshǒu 放手!

453. My goddness!
Tiān na 天哪!

- Na 哪 comes at the end of a sentence to indicate surprise or amazement.

454. Shut up!
Bì zuǐ 闭嘴!

455. No way!
Bù xíng 不行!

🎧456. Nonsense!
Húshuō 胡说!
- Húshuō bā dào 胡说八道 means sheer nonsense, usually more serious than just húshuō 胡说.

457. Nonsense!
Fèihuà 废话!

🎧458. How terrible!
Zhēn kěpà 真可怕!

459. Damn it!
Gāi sǐ le 该死了!

🎧460. Are you sure?
Nǐ kěndìng ma 你肯定吗?

461. Do I have to?
Fēi zuò bù kě ma 非做不可吗?
- Fēi …… bù kě 非 ……不可 is an emphatic expression, meaning must or have to.

🎧462. Are you kidding?
Nǐ zài kāi wánxiào ba 你在开玩笑吧!
- Zài 在 is used as an adverb indicating an action in progress.

463. Oh, you are kidding me.
Ó, nǐ bié ná wǒ kāi wánxiào le 哦, 你别拿我开玩笑了。
- Ó 哦 is used to indicate doubt. Ná 拿 is a preposition introducing the object to be followed by a verbal phrase.

464. You are impatient.

Nǐ tài xìng jí le 你太性急了。

🎧465. You are too confused.
Nǐ tài hútu le 你太糊涂了。

466. You set me up!
Nǐ chūmài wǒ 你出卖我!

🎧467. You're lying.
Nǐ zài sāhuǎng 你在撒谎。

468. You owe me one.
Nǐ qiàn wǒ yí ge rénqíng 你欠我一个人情。

469. You asked for it!
Nǐ zì tǎo kǔ chī 你自讨苦吃!

🎧470. You'd better tell me the truth.
Nǐ gàosù wǒ shíhuà ba 你告诉我实话吧。

471. Control yourself!
Kèzhì yíxià 克制一下。

🎧472. I can't believe it.
Wǒ jiǎnzhí bùgǎn xiāngxìn 我简直不敢相信。

🎧473. Believe it or not!
Xìn bú xìn yóu nǐ 信不信由你!

474. Don't get mad at me.
Nǐ búyào shēng wǒde qì 你不要生我的气。

475. Don't count on me.

Bié zhǐwang wǒ 别指望我。

466476. Don't fall for it!
Bié shàngdàng 别上当!

477. Don't let me down.
Bié ràng wǒ shīwàng 别让我失望。

478. Don't be so modest.
Bié qiānxū le 别谦虚了。

479. Don't get me wrong.
Bié wùhuì wǒ 别误会我。

480. Don't give me that!
Shǎo lái zhè tào 少来这套!

481. Just wait and see!
Děngzhe qiáo 等着瞧!

482. It's gone too far.
Tài lípǔ le 太离谱了。

483. Suit yourself.
Suí nǐde biàn 随你的便。

484. Can you face up to yourself?
Nǐ duìdeqǐ ní zǐjǐ ma 你对得起你自己吗?
- Does this sentence remind you of "I am sorry" duìbuqǐ 对不起?
  Duìbuqǐ 对不起 is literally translated to cannot afford to face.
  Duìdeqǐ 对得起 is its opposite meaning, and is translated to
  "can afford to face", and means to be worthy of.

485. None of your business!

Yǔ nǐ wú guān 与你无关!

🎧486. What are you talking about?
Nǐ zài shuō shénme 你在说什么?

487. What makes you say so?
Nǐ zěnme zhème shuō 你怎么这么说?

488. It's all your fault.
Dōu shì nǐ bù hǎo 都是你不好。
- Dōu 都 is an adverb meaning all, referring to causes.

🎧489. Watch what you are saying.
Shuōhuà yào xiǎoxīn yìdiǎn 说话要小心一点。

490. That's not true.
Nà shì búduì de 那是不对的。

🎧491. That's disgusting.
Zhēn tǎoyàn 真讨厌。

492. That's ridiculous.
Nà tài huāngtáng le 那太荒唐了。

493. You're crazy.
Nǐ fēng le 你疯了。

🎧494. You are conscienceless.
Nǐ méi liángxīn 你没良心。

495. Don't kick up a row.
Búyào wúlǐ qǔ nào 不要无理取闹。

🎧496. You surprised me.

Nǐ ràng wǒ dà chī yī jīng 你让我大吃一惊。

497. You are a chicken.
Nǐ shì ge dǎnxiǎo guǐ 你是个胆小鬼。
- Dǎn 胆 means all bladder, and when it is used as dǎnxiǎo 胆小, it means timid. guǐ 鬼 is a term of abuse.

498. I've had enough.
Wǒ shòugòu le 我受够了。

499. Make up your mind.
Zuò ge juédìng ba 做个决定吧。

500. Can I have a word with you?
Wǒ néng gēn nǐ tán yi tán ma 我能跟你谈一谈吗？

501. It won't take much time.
Bú huì huā hěn duō shíjiān de 不会花很多时间的。

502. It's a waste of time.
Zhè shì làngfèi shíjiān 这是浪费时间。

503. It's absolutely outrageous.
Tài bú xiànghuà le 太不像话了。

504. That's more like it.
Nà yàng cái xiànghuà 那样才像话。

505. That's fair.
Nà yàng gōngpíng 那样公平。

506. Let's make up.
Wǒmen yán guī yú hǎo ba 我们言归于好吧。

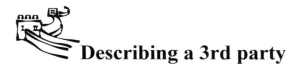# Describing a 3rd party

507. He is my age.

Tā hé wǒ tóng suì 他和我同岁。

508. He was born in New York.

Tā chūshēng zài Niǔ Yuē 他出生在纽约。

> **More: Birth**
> Birthplace: chūshēng dì 出生地
> Birth certificate: chūshēng zhèng 出生证

- Zài 在 is a preposition indicating time, place, condition, scope etc.

509. He always talks big.

Tā zǒngshì chuīniú 他总是吹牛。

510. He lacks courage.

Tā quēfá yǒngqì 他缺乏勇气。

511. He is getting trained on the job.

Tā biān gàn biān xué 他边干边学。

- Biān …… biān…… 边……边…… is used before two verbs respectively to indicate simultaneous actions.

512. She is so smart.

Tā zhēn cōngmíng 她真聪明。

513. She is my best friend.

Tā shì wǒ zuì hǎode péngyou 她是我最好的朋友。

514. She doesn't do make up.

Tā bù huàzhuāng 她不化妆。

🎧515. She is trying to lose weight.
Tā zài jiǎnféi 她在减肥。

516. She doesn't have to (lose weight).
Tā nǎ yǒu féi yào jiǎn 她哪有肥要减?
- • This literally means she doesn't have any fat to lose.

🎧517. She is pregnant.
Tā yǒuxǐ le 她有喜了。

518. She looks like her mom.
Tā xiàng tā māma 她象她妈妈。

🎧519. He is a chip off the old block.
Tā zhǎngde gēn tā bàba yìmú yíyàng
他长得跟他爸爸一模一样。

520. He is left-handed.
Tā shì ge zuǒpiězi 他是个左撇子。

🎧521. He has a sense of humor.
Tā yǒu yōumò gǎn 他有幽默感。

522. He is very popular.
Tā hěn shòu huānyíng 他很受欢迎。

🎧523. He is acting the part of an old man.
Tā zhèng bànyǎn yí ge lǎorén 他正扮演一个老人。

524. He doesn't look tired at all.
Tā kàn qǐlai yìdiǎnr yě bú lèi 他看起来一点儿也不累。

525. He paused for a reply.

Tā tíng xiàlái děngzhe huídá 他停下来等着回答。

- Xiàlái 下来 is used after a verb to indicate completion or result of an action. Zhe 着 also indicates action in progress.

526. This boy has no job.

Zhège nánháir méiyǒu gōngzuò 这个男孩儿没有工作。

- Boy: nánháir 男孩儿 ↔ girl : nǚháir 女孩儿

527. He is looking for a job.

Tā zhèngzài zhǎo gōngzuò 他正在找工作。

- Chinese do not have tenses, but an adverb like zhèngzài 正在 is used to indicate an action in progress.

528. He is fired.

Tā bèi chǎoyóuyú le 他被炒鱿鱼了。

- Chǎoyóuyú 炒鱿鱼 means stir-fry squids. In the old days, you rolled up your mat when you left somewhere, just like squids are rolled up when cooked.

529. He resigned.

Tā chǎole lǎobǎnde yóuyú 他炒了老板的鱿鱼。

- Lǎobǎn 老板 means boss. It means you fired your boss yourself.

530. His company doesn't need him any more.

Tāde gōngsī yòngbuzháo tā le 他的公司用不着他了。

- 着 is read as zháo, which is used after a verb to indicate accomplishment or result.

531. He has a large income.

Tā yǒu hěn gāode shōurù 他有很高的收入。

532. He repairs his house himself.

Tā zìjǐ xiūlǐ zìjǐde fángzi 他自己修理自己的房子。

533. He develops films himself.
Tā zìjǐ chōngxǐ zhàopiàn 他自己冲洗照片。

534. He suggested holding a get-together.
Tā jiànyì bàn yí cì jùhuì 他建议办一次聚会。

535. He can't take a joke.
Tā kāi bùdé wánxiào 他开不得玩笑。
- Bùdé 不得 is used after a verb indicating that such an action cannot or should not be taken.

536. He owes my uncle 100 yuan.
Tā qiàn wǒ shūshu yī bǎi yuán 他欠我叔叔 100 元。

537. He treats me unkindly.
Tā duì wǒ yìdiǎnr dōu bù yǒuhǎo
他对我一点儿都不友好。

538. He is not polite at all.
Tā hěn bú kèqi 他很不客气。
- Here, bú kèqi 不客气 does not mean you are welcome. It describes someone who is polite and courteous.

539. He's very hard on me.
Tā duì wǒ hěn bú kèqi de 他对我很不客气的。

540. He's mean to me.
Tā duì wǒ hěn kēbó 他对我很刻薄。

541. He's very strict.
Tā hěn yánlì 他很严厉。

542. He is collecting money.
Tā zài chóují zījīn 他在筹集资金。

- Zài 在 is an adverb indicating an action is in progress.

543. He won an election.

Tā zài xuǎnjǔzhong huòshēng 他在选举中获胜。

- Zài 在 is a preposition indicating time, place, condition, scope etc.

🎧544. He is very ambitious.

Tāde yěxīn hěn dà 他的野心很大。

545. He's a stranger to me.

Wǒ gēn tā sù bù xiāngshí 我跟他素不相识。

🎧546. These years, they never argued with each other.

Zhè xiē nián, tāmen cóng méi chǎoguo jià, bànguo zuǐ
这些年，他们从没吵过架,拌过嘴.

- Guo 过 comes after a verb indicating completion of action as an experience.

Getting Around

🎧547. Please come up.

Qǐng shànglái 请上来。

 MORE: Action
Come in: jìnlái 进来
Come out: chūlái 出来
Come down: xiàlái 下来
Go down: xiàqù 下去
Go out: chūqù 出去
Go in: jìnqù 进去
Go up: shàngqù 上去

🎧548. Are you all set?
Zhǔnbèi hǎo le ma 准备好了吗?

549. Ready?
Hǎole ma 好了吗?

550. No, not yet.
Hái méi ne 还没呢。

551. Ready.
Zhǔnbèi hǎo le 准备好了。

🎧552. I'll be ready in five minutes.
Wǒ wǔ fēn zhōng jiù hǎo 我 5 分钟就好。

553. This way, please.
Zhèbian qǐng 这边请。

🎧554. After you.
Nǐ xiān qǐng 你先请。

🎧555. Come with me.
Gēn wǒ lái 跟我来。

556. Go this way.
Cóng zhèr zǒu
从这儿走。

MORE: 这儿
Here : zhèli 这里 = zhèr 这儿
There : nàli 那里 = nàr 那儿
Where: nǎli 哪里 = nǎr 哪儿

557. Come on.
Gǎnkuài lái ba 赶快来吧。

🎧558. Let's get going.
Nà wǒmen zǒu ba 那我们走吧。

🎧559. Hold on.
Děng yi děng 等一等。

560. Slow down!
Màn diǎnr 慢点儿!

561. Walk a little slower.
Zǒu màn yìdiǎnr 走慢一点儿。
- When you say yìdiǎnr 一点儿, "n" pronunciation is dropped and roll your tongue as you normally say "r" at the end.

🎧562. Watch out!
Dāngxīn 当心!

🎧563. Be careful!
Zhùyì 注意!

564. Be careful when you cross the road.
Xiǎoxīn guò mǎlù 小心过马路。

🎧565. Please get in (out of) the car.
Qǐng shàng (xià) chē 请上(下)车。

566. Don't move!
Bùxǔ dòng 不许动!

567. Move out of my way!
Ràng kāi 让开!

🎧568. Time is up.
Shíjiān kuàidào le 时间快到了。

569. I'm in a hurry!
Wǒ zài gǎn shíjiān 我在赶时间!

570. Hurry up, we are going to be late.
Nǐ kuài diǎnr, wǒmen gāi chídào le
你快点儿，我们该迟到了。

571. We better take a taxi.
Wǒmen háishì zuò jìchéngchē ba 我们还是坐计程车吧。
- Another common term for taxi is chūzū qìchē 出租汽车。

572. I have to rush!
Wǒ děi gǎnjǐn zǒu 我得赶紧走!

573. Why are you in a hurry?
Wèishénme (gànmá) nàme zhāojí 为什么(干吗)那么着急?
- Gànmá 干吗 is more informal than wèishénme 为什么.

574. What's the hurry?
Jízhe gàn shěnme qù ya 急着干什么去呀?
- Ya 呀 is an interjection indicating surprise.

575. We're going to be late for the movie.
Wǒmen gǎnzhe qù kàn diànyǐng ne
我们赶着去看电影呢。

576. How's the time?
Hái láidejí ma 还来得及吗?
- Láidejí 来得及 means there is still time, or to be able to do something in time.

577. We can't make it, if we don't leave now.
Zài bù zǒu, jiù láibují le 再不走，就来不及了。
- Zài 再 is an adverb indicating continuation of time or action. Láibují 来不及 means there is not enough time, or it's too late. Jiù 就 connects two clauses, the first being the premise of the second.

578. I'll be right there.
Wǒ mǎshàng jiù dào 我马上就到。

 579. Fasten your seat belt.
Xìhǎo nǐde ānquándài 系好你的安全带。
- Hǎo 好 is used after a verb to indicate the completion of an action.

 580. Do you know how to drive?
Nǐ huì kāi chē ma 你会开车吗??

581. I rented a car.
Wǒ zūle yí liàng chē 我租了一辆车。
- Liàng 辆 is a measure word for cars.

 582. This car consumes lots of gas.
Zhè liàng chē tè fèi yóu 这辆车特费油。

583. Did you miss the bus?
Nǐ cuòguo gōnggòng qìchē le 你错过公共汽车了?
- Guo 过 comes after a verb to express the completion of action.

584. I caught the last bus.
Wǒ gǎnshàngle zuì hòu yì bān chē
我赶上了最后一班车。
- Shàng 上 is used after a verb to indicate motion from lower to higher position. Bān 班 is a measure word used to indicate the number of runs in transportation.

 585. What time do you want to leave?
Nǐ xiǎng jǐ diǎn zǒu 你想几点走?

586. What time are we taking off?

Wǒmen jǐ diǎn zǒu 我们几点走?

587. I need to put in some gas before we take off.
Chūfā zhī qián wǒ yào jiā yì diǎn yóu
出发之前我要加一点油。

⏸588. What time do we arrive?
Wǒmen jǐ diǎn néng dào 我们几点能到?

589. In about ten minutes.
Dàyuē shí fēn zhōng yǐhòu 大约 10 分钟以后。

⏸590. How long is the ride?
Zuò chē yào yòng duō cháng shíjiān
坐车要用多长时间?

591. It will take about twenty minutes by bike.
Qí zìxíngchē dàyuē xūyào èr shí fēn zhōng
骑自行车大约需要 20 分钟。

592. Let's talk while we walk.
Wǒmen yìbiān zǒu yìbiān tán 我们一边走一边谈。
 • Yìbiān 一边..... yìbiān 一边..... becomes two different
   verbs to indicate two simultaneous actions.

⏸593. I'm lost.
Wǒ mílù le 我迷路了。

⏸594. Excuse me, can you tell me the way to Tian An Men
Square?
Láojià, qù Tiān Ān Mén Guǎngchǎng zěnme zǒu
劳驾，去天安门广场怎么走?
 • Láojià 劳驾 is a very polite way to say excuse me, meaning
   may I trouble you......

595. Go straight this way.
Xiàng qián zhí zǒu 向前直走。

MORE: Location
Front: qiánmianr 前面儿
Behind: hòumianr 后面儿
Left: zuǒbianr 左边儿
Right: yòubianr 右边儿
Middle zhōngjiān 中间
Inside: lǐbianr 里边儿
Outside: wàibianr 外边儿

🎧596. The road divides here.
Zhè tiáo lù zài zhèli fēnchā
这条路在这里分岔。

- Tiáo 条 is a measure word for something thin and long.

🎧597. Go down this street, then turn left.
Yán zhè tiáo jiē zǒu xiàqù, ránhòu wǎng zuǒ guǎi
沿这条街走下去，然后往左拐。

- Tiáo 条 is a measure word for something thin and long. Xiàqù 下去 is used after a verb to indicate movement from a higher position to a lower one.

598. Turn right at the next crossing.
Zài dì èr ge lùkǒu wǎng yòu guǎi
在第二个路口往右拐。

599. East -West –South-North
Dōng 东- Xī 西- Nán 南 - Běi 北

🎧600. Excuse me, how do I get to the nearest post office?
Qǐngwèn, qù zuì jìnde yóujú zěnme zǒu
请问, 去最近的邮局怎么走?

MORE: How do I get to the .....?
Use qǐngwèn, qù .... zěnme zǒu 请问,
去.......怎么走 format to ask directions.
Airport: jīcháng 机场
Bus Station: gōngchē zhàn 公车站
Subway station: dìxià tiělù zhàn 地下铁路站
Train station: huǒchē zhèn 火车站
Hotel: jiǔdiàn 酒店
Tourist Information Center: lǚyóu zīxūn zhōngxīn
旅游资讯中心

601. Excuse me, is there a bank nearby?
Qǐngwèn, fùjìn yǒu méiyǒu yínháng
请问,附近有没有银行？

MORE: Excuse me, is there..... nearby?
Use qǐngwèn, fùjìn yǒu méiyǒu 请问, 附
近有没有.... format to ask about places.
Department store: bǎihuò gōngsī 百货公司
Travel agency: lǚxíng shè 旅游社
Money exchange: zhǎohuàn diàn 找换店
Hospital: yīyuàn 医院
Restaurant: cāntīng 餐厅
Coffee shop: kāfēi diàn 咖啡店
Bar: jiǔba 酒吧
Drug store: yàodiàn 药店

602. Where is the toilet?
Xǐshǒujiān zài nǎr   洗手间在哪儿？
• Public toilet is called gōnggòng cèsuǒ 公共厕所.

603. I'm sorry. I have no idea where it is.
Duìbuqǐ, wǒ bù zhīdào tā zài nǎr
对不起，我不知道它在哪儿。

604. Thank you anyway.

Jìnguǎn rúcǐ, háishì yào xièxiè nǐ
尽管如此，还是要谢谢你。

605. Oh no, I got a flat tire on my bike.
Āiyā, wóde zìxíngchē bàotái le
哎呀，我的自行车爆胎了。
  • Āiyā 哎呀 is an interjection showing surprise.

606. Is it far from here?
Lí zhèr yuǎn ma 离这儿远吗？

607. No, it's just over there.
Bù yuǎn, jiùzài nàli 不远，就在那里。

608. It's near here.
Lí zhèr hěn jìn 离这儿很近。

609. Just around the corner.
Jiù zài fùjìn 就在附近。

610. It's about one kilometer from here.
Jù zhèli yuē yī gōngli 距这里约 1 公里。

611. It's far. You'd better take a bus.
Yuǎn, nǐ zuì hǎo zuò gōnggòng qìchē qù
远，你最好坐公共汽车去。

612. There comes a bus.
Qìchē lái le 汽车来了。

613. Excuse me, does bus No. 4 stop at
Wang Fu Jing?
Qǐngwèn, sì lù chē qù Wáng Fǔ Jǐng ma
请问，4 路车去王府井吗？

614. Do I have to change buses to Wang Fu Jing?
Qù Wáng Fǔ Jǐng yào huàn chē ma 去王府井要换车吗?

615. How many stops to Wang Fu Jing?
Dào Wáng Fǔ Jǐng háiyou jǐ zhàn 到王府井还有几站?

🎧616. You can't miss it
Nǐ yídìng néng zhǎodào de 你一定能找到的。
- Dào 到 is used after a verb as an compliment to indicate success.

🎧617. Show me.
Zhǐ gěi wǒ kàn 指给我看。

618. I'll show you.
Wǒ zhǐ gěi nǐ kàn 我指给你看。

🎧619. I'll take you there.
Wǒ dài nǐ qù ba 我带你去吧。

620. There are too many people here.
Zhèli rén hěn duō 这里人很多。

621. I don't know anybody.
Wǒ yí ge rén dōu bú rènshi 我一个人都不认识。

🎧622. There you are!
À, yuánlái nǐ zài zhèr 啊, 原来你在这儿!
- À 啊 ia an interjection expressing sudden realization.

🎧623. Are you looking for me?
Nǐ zhǎo wǒ ma 你找我吗?

🎧624. Have you seen Cheng?

Nǐ jiàndào xiǎo Chéng ma 你见到小城吗?

> **MORE: Forms of Address**
> The most common term between close relationships is ā 阿, which is used before a family name or part of a given name. It can be used before a title or family name and other relationships including a pet's name as well. For example, for someone named Chén dé míng 陈德明, his family member and close friends would call him ā míng 阿明, and at work he might be called ā Chén 阿陈. In non-family acquaintances, Chinese people are generally referred to by their last name followed by a title.
> When calling: last name + title
> Formal or written occasions: last name + given name + title
> Mr., Sir. : xiānsheng 先生
> Miss, Ms., Mrs. : xiǎojie 小姐
> Lady, Mrs. : nǚshi 女士
> Manager : jīnglǐ 经理
> Master : shīfu 师傅 (originally it was for a skilled person such as a cook, carpenter, or plumber, but now its usage has expanded to even calling a stranger.)
> Teacher : lǎoshī 老师 (it's for teachers as well as someone intellectual.)
> Ladies and gentlemen: nǚshìmen xiānshēngmen 女士们, 先生们。
> Friends usually go by their personal names, but a popular way to address each other among Chinese, regardless of gender, is to add an age-related term of honor before the family name, such as xiǎo Wáng 小王 and dà gē 大哥.
> Lǎo 老: Means old. For elderly people.
> Xiǎo 小: Means young. For someone younger.
> Dà 大: Means elder. For someone older than yourself.

625. No, not today.
Méiyǒu, jīntiān méi kànjiàn tā 没有，今天没看见他。

626. He was here a few minutes ago.
Jǐ fēn zhōng qián tā hái zài zhèr lái zhe
几分钟前他还在这儿来着。

🎧627. Do you see him often?

Nǐ jīngcháng jiàndào tā ma 你经常见到他吗？

628. I ran into him.
Wǒ ǒurán pèngdàole tā 我偶然碰到了他。

 **On the Phone**

629. Hello?
Wèi 喂？
- In many parts of China, this is also said in 2nd tone.

630. Is Cheng there?
Xiǎo Chéng zài ma 小城在吗？

631. May I speak to Cheng ?
Wǒ kěyǐ zhǎo xiǎo Chéng jiē diànhuà ma
我可以找小城接电话吗？

632. Speaking.
Wǒ jiùshì 我就是。

633. What are you doing now?
Xiànzài nǐ zuò shénme ne 现在你做什么呢？
- Ne 呢 is a particle used at the end of an interrogative sentence.

634. I am taking a rest.
Wǒ zài xiūxi ne 我在休息呢。
- Ne 呢 is a particle used at the end of statement to give emphasis.

🎧635. Who's calling?
Shì nǎ yí wèi 是哪一位?

636. I'll get it.
Wǒ qù jiē diànhuà 我去接电话。

🎧637. Extension 123 please.
Qǐng zhuǎn yī èr sān fēnjī 请转 123 分机。

🎧638. Hold on, please.
Shāo děng yíxià 稍等一下。

639. Here is a call for you.
Yǒu nǐde diànhuà 有你的电话。

🎧640. Sorry, he's not here.
Duìbuqǐ, tā búzài 对不起，他不在。

641. He doesn't have time.
Tā méi kòng 他没空。

🎧642. Any messages for me?
Yǒu wǒde liúyán ma
有我的留言吗?

643. May I leave a message?
Wǒ néng liú ge kǒuxìn ma
我能留个口信吗?

644. Can I take a message for him?
Wǒ néng dài shōu ge kǒuxìn ma 我能代收口信吗?

🎧645. Can I take a message?

Yào wǒ chuánhuà ma 要我传话吗？

🎧646. Don't bother.
Búyòng máfán le 不用麻烦了。

🎧647. Have him return my call.
Ràng tā gěi wǒ huí diànhuà 让他给我回电话。

648. I'll tell him.
Wǒ huì zhuǎngào tā 我会转告他。

649. I was just about to call you.
Wǒ zhèng zhǔnbèi dǎ diànhuà gěi nǐ
我正准备打电话给你。

🎧650. You've dialed the wrong number.
Nǐ bō cuò diànhuà hàomǎ le
你拨错电话号码了。

• Mǎ 码 and ma 吗 look similar but their radicals are different.
  Mǎ 码= 石 (means rock) + 马 (means horse)
  Ma 吗 = 口 (means mouth) + 马(means horse)

651. Call me tomorrow.
Míngtiān dǎ diànhuà gěi wǒ 明天打电话给我。

652. Give me a call.
Gěi wǒ dǎ diànhuà 给我打电话。

🎧653. Let me call you back later.
Wǒ guò yìhuìr dǎgěi nǐ ba 我过一会儿打给你吧。

Household Expressions

654. Time to get up!
Gāi qǐchuáng le 该起床了!

655. I don't want to (get up).
Wǒ zhēn bù xiǎng qǐ 我真不想起。

656. I'm still yawning.
Wǒ hái dǎ hāqian ne 我还打哈欠呢。

657. I'm still sleepy.
Wǒ hái kùnzhe ne 我还困着呢!

658. Hurry get up!
Kuài diǎnr qǐchuáng 快点儿起床!

659. Are you awake?
Nì xǐngle ma 你醒了吗?

660. I am now.
Wǒ gāng xǐng 我刚醒。

661. Can you turn off the alarm clock?
Néng bāng wǒ guāndiào nàozhōng ma
能帮我关掉闹钟吗?

- Diào 掉 is used as a complement indicating disposal.

662. Please turn off the alarm clock.
Qǐng bǎ nàozhōng guān le 请把闹钟关了。

663. Did the alarm clock go off?
Nàozhōng xiǎngle ma 闹钟响了吗?

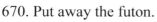664. Not a sound was heard.
Yìdiǎn shēngyīn yě méiyǒu 一点声音也没有。

665. You are finally up.
Nǐ zhōngyú qǐlái le 你终于起来了。

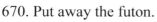666. Did you stay up late last night?
Zuówǎn nǐ áoyè le 昨晚你熬夜了?

667. You didn't turn the the light off.
Nǐ yìzhí méi guān dēng a 你一直没关灯啊。
- A 啊 is used at the end of a sentence to convey an undertone of warning. Méi 没 is another negative adverb but mainly used to negate 有 meaning "there is or there are". The shortened form of méi 没 instead of méiyǒu 没有 is common as well. Here méi 没 is used to form the negation of a completed action.

668. You forgot to turn off the light.
Nǐ wàngle guān dēng le 你忘了关灯了。

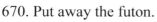669. Let's fold up the futon.
Bǎ bèizi dié hǎo 把被子叠好。
- Hǎo 好 is used after a verb to indicate the completion of an action.

670. Put away the futon.
Bǎ bèizi shōu qǐlái ba 把被子收起来吧。
- Qǐlái 起来 is used as a complement after a verb indicating upward movement.

671. You were sawing logs last night.
Zuótiān wǎngshang nǐ dǎ hūlu le 昨天晚上你打呼噜了。

🎧672. Did I keep you up?
Yǐngxiǎng nǐ shuìjiàole ma 影响你睡觉了吗?

673. I need to wash my face.
Wǒ děi xǐ liǎn le 我得洗脸了。

🎧674. I had a bad dream.
Wǒ zuòle ge kěpàde mèng 我做了个可怕的梦。

🎧675. It's alright now.
Xiànzài méi shì le 现在没事了。

🎧676. Did you brush your teeth?
Shuā yá le ma 刷牙了吗?
- Yáshuā 牙刷 means toothbrush.

677. I need to comb my hair.
Wǒ děi shū shū tóu le 我得梳梳头了。
- Shūzi 梳子 means comb.

678. Put away your pajamas.
Bǎ shuìyī shōu hǎo 把睡衣收好。

🎧679. Go get changed.
Kuài qù huàn yīfu 快去换衣服。

680. Open the window.
Dǎkāi chuānghu 打开窗户。

🎧681. What am I going to wear today?
Jīntiān chuān shénme hǎo ne 今天穿什么好呢?

682. The red one.
Chuān hóngde ba 穿红的吧!

MORE: Color
Red: hóng 红
Green: lǜ 绿
Yellow: huáng 黄
White: bái 白
Black: hēi 黑

683. Oh, I am going to wash it.
Ā, wǒ zhèng yào xǐ ne
啊，我正要洗呢。

684. You're wearing your sweater inside out.
Máoyī chuān fǎn le 毛衣穿反了。

685. Pick it up.
Bǎ tā jiǎn qǐlai 把它捡起来。

686. Roll it up.
Bǎ tā juǎn qǐlai 把它卷起来。

687. Lift it up.
Bǎ tā jǔ qǐlai 把它举起来。

688. Wrap it up.
Bǎ tā bāo qǐlai 把它包起来。

689. Stand up.
Zhàn qǐlai 站起来。

690. I need to sweep the floor.
Wǒ yào sǎo dì 我要扫地。

691. Time for breakfast.
Gāi chī zǎofàn le 该吃早饭了。

🎧692. Are you gonna be late today?
Nǐ jīntiān huì huíláide wǎn ma 你今天会回来得晚吗?

- Huì 会 means be likely to. De 得 is used between a verb and its compliment to indicate degree.

🎧693. No, I'll be home at the usual time.
Bù, hé píngcháng yíyàng 不，和平常一样。

694. What time are you coming home?
Jǐ diǎn huílái 几点回来?

695. Around seven o'clock.
Dàgài qī diǎn zuǒyòu ba 大概 7 点左右吧。

696. Don't forget to bring something back for me.
Bié wàngle gěi wǒ dài diǎnr shénme
别忘了给我带点儿什么。

697. Don't worry, I won't.
Fàngxīn ba, wàngbuliǎo 放心吧，忘不了。

🎧698. Don't forget to lock the door when you leave.
Chūménde shíhou, kě bié wàng le suǒ mén
出门的时候，可别忘了锁门。

699. Did you lock the door?
Nǐ suǒ mén le ma 你锁门了吗?

🎧700. Look, I forgot to turn the gas off on the stove.
Nǐ kàn kàn wǒ, bǎ wǎsī guāndiào dōu gěi wàng le
你看看我，把瓦斯关掉都给忘了。

- Gěi 给 is used before the main verb of the sentence, usually with bǎ 把 for emphasis.

🎧701. Have you got your lunch box?
Fànhé dài le ma 饭盒带了吗？

702. Yes, right here.
Ng, dài le 嗯，带了。
- Ng 嗯 is an interjection indicating response.

703. I'm leaving, Mom.
Wǒ zǒule, māma 我走了，妈妈。

🎧704. It might rain today.
Jīntiān hǎoxiàng yào xiàyǔ 今天好像要下雨。

🎧705. Take your umbrella with you.
Dàishàng sǎn ba 带上伞吧!
- Shàng 上 is used after a verb to indicate from a lower to higher position. Giving an umbrella for a present is a taboo in China. Because sǎn 伞 and sàn 散 ,meaning break up, rhyme.

706. Didn't forget anything, did you?
Méi wàngle shénme dōngxi ba 没忘了什么东西吧?

707. I don't think so.
Wǒ xiǎng méiyǒu 我想没有。

🎧708. Hurry up!
Kuài diǎnr ba 快点儿吧!

709. Mom, if only I could fly.
Māma, yàoshì wǒ néng fēi jiù hǎo le
妈妈，要是我能飞就好了。

🎧710. I'm home.
Wǒ huílái le 我回来了。

🎧711. I'll be back soon.
Wǒ mǎshàng huílái 我马上回来。

712. I'll be right there.
Wǒ mǎshàng jiù qù 我马上就去。

713. I'm on my way.
Wǒ zhè jiù shànglù 我这就上路。
- Shàng 上 is a verb meaning go to, or leave for. Zhè 这 means this moment or now.

🎧714. He is on his way.
Tā xiànzài yǐjīng zài lùshàng le 他现在已经在路上了。
- Shang 上 is used after nouns to indicate the surface of an object.

🎧715. I'm tired.
Zhēn lèi a 真累啊!
- A 啊 is used at the end of a sentence to convey an undertone of warning.

716. I'm exhausted.
Wǒ jīng pí lì jìn le 我精疲力尽了。

🎧717. You need to workout.
Nǐ xūyào qù yùndòng duànliàn yíxià
你需要去运动锻炼一下。

718. What do you want for dinner?
Wǎnfàn nǐ xiǎng chī shénme 晚饭你想吃什么?

719. Let's make dumplings together.
Jīnwǎn wǒmen yìqǐ bāo jiǎozi ba
今晚我们一起包饺子吧。

🎧720. Would you run to the store?
Nǐnéng bù néng kuài diǎnr qù tàng shāngdiàn
你能不能快点儿去趟商店?
  • Tàng 趟 is a measure word for trip.

🎧721. In a minute.
Shāo děng yíxià 稍等一下。

🎧722. I want to take a shower first.
Wǒ yào xiān chōng ge zǎo 我要先冲个澡。

🎧723. Is dinner ready?
Wǎnfàn hǎo le ma 晚饭好了吗?

724. Not yet.
Hái méi ne 还没呢。

725. Supper is ready at six.
Wǎncān liù diǎnzhōng jiù hǎo le 晚餐六点钟就好了。

🎧726. I'm starving!
Wǒ è sǐ le 我饿死了。

727. How soon can you get it ready?
Hái yào duōjiǔ cái néng zuǒ hǎo ya 还要多久才能做好呀?

728. In about five more minutes.
Zài yǒu wǔ fēnzhōng ba 再有 5 分钟吧。

🎧729. Please go ahead.
Qǐng xiān chī ba 请先吃吧。

730. Breakfast/Lunch/Dinner is ready!

Zǎofàn/ wǔfàn / wǎnfàn hǎo le a
早饭/ 午饭/ 晚饭好了啊!

- A 啊 is used at the end of a sentence to convey an undertone of warning.

731. Would you help me set the table?
Nǐ bāng wǒ zhǔnbèi cānjù hǎo ma 你帮我准备餐具, 好吗?

 MORE:Tableware
Bowl : wǎn 碗
Plate：diézi 碟子
Fork：chāzi 叉子
Spoon：tāngchí 汤匙
Knife：dāozi 刀子
Chopsticks：kuàizi 筷子
Napkin: cānjīn 餐巾

732. Did you wash your hands well?
Shǒu xǐ gānjìng le ma 手洗干净了吗?

- Gānjìng 干净 means clean.

 MORE: Body Parts
Head: tóu 头
Hair: tóufa 头发
Eyes: yǎnjīng 眼睛
Nose: bízi 鼻子
Ears: érduo 耳朵
Mouth: zuǐba 嘴巴
Neck: bózi 脖子
Leg: tuǐ 腿

733. Don't spill it!
Bié nòng sǎ le 别弄洒了。

734. Finish up your plate.
Bǎ fàn chī gānjìng 把饭吃干净。

- Gānjìng 干净 means totally or completely as an adverb.

735. I'm trying to.
Zhè bù chīzhe ne ma 这不吃着呢嘛。
- Ma 嘛 is used at the end of a sentence to show what precedes is obvious.

736. I don't like vegetables.
Wǒ bù xǐhuan chī shūcài
我不喜欢吃蔬菜。

MORE: Vegetables
Asparagus: lúsǔn 芦笋
Carrot: hóng luóbo 红萝卜
Cabbage: juǎnxīn cài 卷心菜
Bok Choy: xiǎobái cài 小白菜
Bean Sprout: dòu yá 豆芽

737. Don't be picky.
Bùxǔ tiāoshí 不许挑食。

738. This knife cuts well, doesn't it?
Zhè dāo tǐng hǎoshǐ de, shì búshì 这刀挺好使的, 是不是?

739. It sure does.
Zhēn tǐng kuài de 真挺快的。

740. Would you put the dishes away?
Néng bāng wǒ shōushi pánzi ma 能帮我收拾盘子吗?

741. What are you doing?
Nǐ zài gànmá 你在干吗?

742. I'm ironing my shirt
Wǒ zài yùn chènshān ne

我在熨衬衫呢。
- Yùndǒu 熨斗 means iron.

743. I was just daydreaming.
Wǒ zhǐshì fāle huìr dāi 我只是发了会儿呆。

744. I'm just killing time.
Wǒ zhǐshì zài xiāomó shíjiān 我只是在消磨时间。

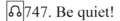745. I was just thinking.
Wǒ zài xiǎng diǎnr shì 我在想点儿事。

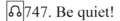746. Don't cry.
Búyào kū 不要哭。

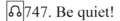747. Be quiet!
Ānjìng diǎn 安静点!
- Diǎn 点 is a measure word meaning a little or some.

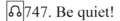748. Quiet down!
Búyào nào 不要闹。
- This is mostly said by parents to their kids.

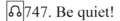749. Don't fight!
Bié dǎ le 别打了!

750. Don't argue anymore!
Bié zhēng le 别争了!

751. What are you guys up to?
Nǐmen liǎ gǎo shénme guǐ 你们俩搞什么鬼?
- Gǎoguǐ 搞鬼 means to be up to something mischievous.

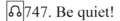752. Rock, paper, scissors!

Jiǎndāo, shítou, bù 剪刀，石头，布。

- It literally means scissors, rock, cloth.

753. Here you are.
Gěi nǐ 给你。

754. I'll fix you up.
Wǒ huì bāng nǐ dǎdiǎn de 我会帮你打点的。

755. Take your time.
Mànmànr lái 慢慢儿来。

756. Please don't disturb me.
Qǐng bié dǎrǎo wǒ 请别打扰我。

757. I can't hear you very well.
Wǒ tīng bu qīngchu nǐ shuōde huà
我听不清楚你说的话。

758. Speak louder，please.
Shuōhuà qǐng dà shēng diǎnr 说话请大声点儿。

759. Is Mr. Zhang around?
Zhāng xiānsheng zài ma 张先生在吗?

760. I want to speak with him.
Wǒ xiǎng gēn tā shuōhuà 我想跟他说话。

761. Please come in.
Qǐng jìn 请进。

762. You are just in time.
Nǐ láide zhèng shì shíhou 你来得正是时候。

763. Oh, this is not a good time for us.
Āiyā, nǐ láide zhēn búshì shíhou
哎呀， 你来得真不是时候。

- Āiyā哎呀 is an interjection showing surprise.

764. Welcome (to our house).
Huānyíng huānyíng　欢迎欢迎。

765. Please have a seat.
Qǐng zuò 请坐。

766. Please have some tea.
Qǐng hē chá 请喝茶。

767. Make yourself at home.
Qǐng búyào jūlǐ 请不要拘礼。

768. Sister, do me a favor?
Jiějie, bāng ge máng hǎo ma 姐姐, 帮个忙好吗?

- In a Chinese family, elder family members are usually called by their titles, and children can be called by their given name or nicknames. But even within siblings, the relationship is clearly stressed by their gender and age.

769. Give me a hand!
Bāng bāng wǒ 帮帮我!

770. Oh no, that wasn't helpful at all.
Āiyā , nǐ zhēn bāng dàománg le 哎呀, 你真帮倒忙了。

- Bāng dàománg 帮倒忙 means do somebody disservice.

771. Allow me.
Ràng wǒ lái 让我来。

772. It's your turn.

Lún dào ní le 轮到你了。

773. Oh no, I can't push it. I can't pull it either.
Āiyā, tuī yě tuī bú dòng, lā yě lā bú dòng
哎呀, 推也推不动, 拉也拉不动。

774. My car needs to be washed.
Wǒde chē xūyào xǐ yi xǐ 我的车需要洗一洗。

> **MORE: Car Brands**
> Car brands are really named with a transliteration of good meanings. Look at the examples.
> Benz: Bēn chí 奔驰 (bēnchí 奔驰 means run fast.)
> Ford: Fú tè 福特 (fortune-special)
> Chevy: Xuě tiè lóng 雪铁龙 (snow-metal-dragon)
> Volvo: Wò ěr wò 沃尔沃 (rich-you-rich)
> BMW: Bǎo mǎ 宝马 (treasure-horse)
> Japanese and Koreans brands which already have Chinese characters are called in Chinese own pronunciation.
> Toyoda:Fēng tián 丰田
> Honda: Běn tián 本田
> Mistubishi: Sān líng 三菱
> Hyundai: Siàn dēi 现代
> Daewoo: Dà yú 大宇

775. Can you help me hang this picture?
Nǐ bāng wó guà zhè fú huà, hǎo ma
你帮我挂这幅画, 好吗?
   •   Fú 幅 is a measure word for clothing or painting.

776. It's upside down.
Shàng xià diāndǎo le 上下颠倒了。

777. Don't forget to throw the trash away.
Bié wàngle rēng lājī ya 别忘了扔垃圾呀。

778. I won't.
Wàngbuliǎo 忘不了!

779. This house is my own.
Zhè suǒ fángzi shì wǒ zìjǐ de 这所房子是我自己的。
- Suǒ 所 is a measure word for buildings.

780. The water is boiling!
Shuǐ kāi la 水开啦!
- La 啦 is the representation of the combined sounds "le" and "a", denoting exclamation and interrogation etc.

781. I know!
Zhīdào la 知道啦!

782. Don't be so childish.
Bié zhème háizi qì 别这么孩子气。

783. He is just a child.
Tā zhǐshì ge háizi 他只是个孩子。

784. He is a smart boy.
Tā shì ge xiǎo jīling guǐ 他是个小机灵鬼。
- Xiǎoguǐ 小鬼 means little devil, and it's a term of endearment in addressing a child.

785. Can I go out to play?
Wǒ kěyǐ chūqù wánr huìr ma
我可以出去玩儿会儿吗?

786. After you finish your homework.
Xiěwán zuòyè zài qù ba
写完作业再去吧。

787. I'm going to cram school now.
Wǒ qù bǔxí xuéxiào le a 我去补习学校了啊。
- A 啊 is used at the end of a sentence to convey an undertone of warning.

788. Study hard.
Hǎohǎor xuéxí a 好好儿学习啊!

789. Let's play hooky today!
Jīntiān wǒmen táoxué ba 今天我们逃学吧。

790. May I have my allowance?
Néng gěi wǒ diǎnr língyòng qián ma
能给我点儿零用钱吗?

791. What do you want to buy?
Nǐ yào mǎi shénme yā 你要买什么呀?
- Yā 呀 is an interjection indicating surprise.

792. I play ball after school.
Xiàkè hòu wǒ qù dǎqiú 下课后我去打球。

793. Why don't you have some snacks?
Chī diǎnr diǎnxin ba 吃点儿点心吧。

794. Where are the snacks?
Diǎnxin zài nǎr 点心在哪儿?

795. They're in the cupboard.
Zài wǎnchú li 在碗橱里。

796. There are watermelons in the refrigerator.
Yǒu xīguā zài bīngxiāngli 有西瓜在冰箱里。

MORE: Fruits
Pear: lízi 梨子
Grapes: pútáo 葡萄
Peach: táozi 桃子
Kiwi :qíyìguǒ 奇异果
Lychee: lìzhī 荔枝
Banana: xiāngjiāo 香蕉
Strawberry: cáoměi 草莓

🎧797. Take it easy!
Fàngsōng diǎnr 放松点儿!

798. I can't. I have a test tomorrow.
Bù kěnéng, wǒ míngtiān yào kǎoshì
不可能，我明天要考试。

🎧799. Let's review it together.
Wǒmen yìqǐ fùxí yíxià ba 我们一起复习一下吧。

800. 1 plus 2 equals 3.
Yī jiā èr shì sān 一加二是三。
- Jiā fǎ 加法 means addition.

801. How much is 20 minus 3?
Èr shí jiǎn sān shì duōshao 二十减三是多少?
- Jiǎn fǎ 减法 means subtraction.

🎧802. What are you doing today?
Jīntiān nǐ gàn shénme 今天你干什么?

🎧803. We're having a track and field meet.
Jīntiān wǒmen kāi yùndòng huì
今天我们开运动会。

804. I am learning to play piano.

Wǒ zài xué tán gāngqín 我在学弹钢琴。

805. Do re mi fa sol ra si do
Duō léi mǐ fā suǒ lā sī duō
多雷米發索拉西多。

806. She went to school.
Tā shàngxué qù le 她上学去了。

807. Is this your pen?
Zhèshì nǐde bǐ ma 这是你的笔吗?

808. May I borrow your pen?
Wǒ kěyǐ jièyòng nǐde bǐ ma
我可以借用你的笔吗?

809. Zhang Cheng (student), who is in your family?
Zhāng Chéng tóngxué, nǐ jiā yǒu shéi
张城同学, 你家有谁?

810. I have dad, mom, an older brother and a younger sister.
Wǒ yǒu bāba, māma, gēge hé mèimei
我有爸爸, 妈妈, 哥哥和妹妹。

811. My granddaughter went to visit her teacher.
Wǒde sūnnǚ qù bàifǎng tāde lǎoshī le
我的孙女去拜访她的老师了。

812. We are moving in two weeks.
Wǒmen liǎng ge xīngqī zhī hòu bānjiā
我们两个星期之后搬家。

 **Shopping**

813. What do you want?
Ní yào shénme 你要什么?

814. How much are the apples for a jin?
Píngguǒ duōshao qián yì jīn 苹果多少钱一斤?
- One jīn 斤 is 500 g, about 1.1lbs. In traditional markets, most of things are still sold by weight, like meat, rice, fruits, vegetables, eggs, even fabrics!

815. It's two fifty for a jin.
Yì jīn liǎng kuài wǔ 一斤两块五。

816. Taste some.
Cháng yi cháng ba 尝一尝吧。

817. It's very good.
Hěn hǎochī 很好吃。

818. How much do you want?
Ní yào duōshao 你要多少?

819. I want 3 jin apples and 2 jin tangerines.
Wǒ yào sān jīn píngguǒ gēn liǎng jīn júzi
我要三斤苹果跟两斤橘子。

820. May I help you?
Wǒ néng bāng ní ma 我能帮你吗?

🎧821. Is there anything you would like?
Nín yào mǎi shénme 您要买什么？

822. Which one would you prefer?
Ní yào xuǎn nǎ yí ge 你要选哪个？

🎧823. I am just looking.
Wǒ zhǐshì suíbiàn kànkàn 我只是随便看看。

824. Yes, I'd like to buy a book.
Shìde, wǒ yào mǎi běn shū
是的，我要买本书。

- Běn 本 is a measure word for books.

🎧825. I want to buy a shirt.
Wǒ xiǎng mǎi yí jiàn chènshān 我想买一件衬衫。

- 件 jiàn is a measure word for clothing.

MORE: Clothings
Pants: kùzi 裤子
Skirts: qúnzi 裙子
Coats: dàyī 大衣
Blue jeans: niúzǎi kù 牛仔裤
Suits: zhèngzhuāng 正装
Windbreaker: fēngyī 风衣
Rain jacket: yǔyī 雨衣

🎧826. What color/size/style do you want?
Yào shénme yánsè/ chìcūn/ yàngzi de
要什么颜色 / 尺寸 / 样子的？

827. A blue one.
Lánsè de 蓝色的。

828. What size shoes would you like?

Ní yào jǐ hàode xié 你要几号的鞋?

MORE: Size

Men's clothing

US	S	M	L	XL	XXL
Europe	44	46~48	50	52~54	
China	S	M	L	XL	XXL

Women's clothing

US	4	6	8	10	12	14
Europe	34	36	38	40	42	44
China	S	M	M-L	L	XL	XXL

Men's shoes

US	8	8.5	9	9.5	10	10.5	11
Europe	41	42	43	43.5	44	44.5	45
China	42	43	43.5	44	44.5	45	46

Women's shoes

US	6.5	7	7.5	8	8.5	9
Europe	37	37.5	38	38.5	39	40
China	37.5	38	39	39.5	40	41

829. Can I try it on?
Kěyǐ shìchuān ma 可以试穿吗？

830. Sure, fitting room is over there.
Kěyǐ, gèngyīshì zài nàbian
可以, 更衣室在那边。

831. Do you have one size smaller (bigger)?

Yǒu méiyǒu xiǎo (dà) yí hào de 有没有小(大)一号的？

🎧832. Do you have any other styles?
Yǒu méiyǒu biéde kuǎnshì 有没有别的款式？

833. I like it very much.
Wǒ fēicháng xǐhuan 我非常喜欢。

🎧834. All right. I'll take it.
Hǎode, wǒ mǎi zhè jiàn ba 好的，我买这件吧。

835. Any thing else?
Hái yào biéde ma 还要别的吗？

836. That's all!
Jiù zhèyàng 就这样！

🎧837. That's all I need.
Wǒ jiù yào zhè xiē 我就要这些。

838. I'm broke.
Wǒ shēn wú fēn wén 我身无分文。

🎧839. How much is it?
Duōshao qián 多少钱？

🎧840. It's seventeen yuan and five mao.
Shí qī kuài wǔ máo (qián) 十七块五毛(钱)。
• Chinese currency is RMB ￥ Rén Mín Bì 人民币. Yuán 元 is the monetry unit of China, but colloquially kuài 块 is used. Máo 毛 is 1/10 of a yuán 元.

🎧841. It's too expensive.
Tài guì le 太贵了。

🎧842. Could you make it cheaper?
Kěyǐ piányi yīdiǎn ma 可以便宜点吗？

843. What a good deal!
Zhēn piányi 真便宜!

🎧844. Where do I pay?
Zài nǎr fùkuǎn 在哪儿付款？

845. You pay at the cashier over there.
Nín kěyǐ zài nàbiande shōuyíntái fùkuǎn
您可以在那边的收银台付款

846. Do you want to pay by cash or credit card?
Nínyào fù xiànjīn háishì yòng xìnyòng kǎ
您要付现金还是用信用卡？

🎧847. May I use a credit card?
Wǒ néng shǐyòng xìnyòng kǎ ma 我能使用信用卡吗？
- Kǎ 卡 is a transliteration of card.

848. It really comes in handy.
Yǒule tā zhēnshì fāngbiàn 有了它真是方便。

849. It won't work.
Xíng bu tōng 行不通。

850. Do you have any other credit card?
Yǒu méiyǒu qítāde xìnyòng kǎ 有没有其他的信用卡？

851. May I pay by installments?
Wǒ kěyǐ fēnqī fùkuǎn ma 我可以分期付款吗？

🎧852. I forgot to bring my VIP card.

Wǒ wàngle dài guìbīn kǎ 我忘了带贵宾卡。

🎧853. Can I get 10% off?
Nǐ jiù dǎ jiǔ zhé yōuhuì ba 你就打 9 折优惠吧。
- Zhé 折 means discount. Pay attention to saying percentage in Chinese. Dǎ jiǔ zhé 打 9 折 is 10% off, so 20% off is dǎ bā zhé 打 8 折.

🎧854. Do you have some change?
Nǐ yǒu língqián ma 你有零钱吗？

855. Here's your change.
Zhè shì zhǎo nínde qián 这是找您的钱。

856. Here is your receipt.
Zhè shì gěi nínde shōujù 这是给您的收据。

857. Thanks for your good service.
Xièxiè nǐde rèqíng fúwù 谢谢你的热情服务。

🎧858. Do come again, please.
Huānyíng zài lái 欢迎再来。

 **At a Restaurant**

859. Let's have something to drink.
Wǒmen hē diǎnr shénme ba
我们喝点儿什么吧。

🎧860. Would you care for a drink?
Nǐ yào búyào lái diǎnr hē de

你要不要来点儿喝的?

🎧861. I would like a cup of coffee, please.
Qǐng gěi wǒ yì bēi kāfēi 请给我一杯咖啡。

862. Do you want sugar and cream with it?
Jiā bù jiā táng hé nǎi 加不加糖和奶?

 MORE: Drinks 1
Water: shuǐ 水
Mineral water: kuàngquán shuǐ 矿泉水
Fruit juice: guǒzhī 果汁
Apple juice: píngguǒzhī 苹果汁
Orange juice: chéngzhī 橙汁
Coca cola: kěkǒu kělè 可口可乐
Pepsi cola: bǎishì kělè 百事可乐
Fanta: fēndá 芬达
Sprite: xuěbì 雪碧
7-up: qīxǐ 七喜
Milk: niúnǎi 牛奶
Cocoa:kěkě 可可

🎧863. I'll treat you to dinner.
Wǒ xiǎng qǐng nǐ chī wǎnfàn 我想请你吃晚饭。

864. I appreciate your invitation.
Gǎnxiè nǐde yāoqǐng 感谢你的邀请。

🎧865. Let's celebrate!
Wǒmen hǎohǎor qìngzhù yíxià ba
我们好好儿庆祝一下吧!

🎧866. Can I take a rain check?
Nǐ néng gǎitiān zài qǐng wǒ ma 你能改天再请我吗?

🎧867. Welcome!
Huānyíng guānglín 欢迎光临!
- If you go to restaurants or stores, the first thing you may hear, or the first sign you will see might be "welcome" huānyíng guānglín 欢迎光临, which literally means we joyfully welcome your gracious arrival.

🎧868. How late are you open?
Nǐmen yíngyè dào jǐdiǎn 你们营业到几点?

869. Till 3 am.
Dào língchén sān diǎn 到零晨 3 点。

🎧870. Let's talk while eating.
Wǒmen biān chī biān tán ba 我们边吃边谈吧。

871. My treat.
Wǒ qǐng kè 我请客。
- Read it as wǒ 我 (2nd tone) + qǐng 请 (half 3rd tone) + kè 客 (4th tone).

🎧872. Dinner is on me.
Wǎnfàn wǒ qǐng kè 晚饭我请客。

873. It's on me. (Treating one person)
Wǒ qǐng nǐ 我请你。
- Read it as wǒ 我(half 3rd tone) + qǐng 请(2nd tone) + nǐ 你(3rd tone).

874. For here or to go?
Zài zhèr chī háishì dàizǒu
在这儿吃还是带走?

🎧875. I'm hungry
Wǒ è le 我饿了。

- Even though the Chinese language doesn't have tenses, a particle like le 了 can effectively deliver the meaning of completion or change. In wǒ è le 我饿了, le 了 indicates change that now I am hungry.

876. Please show me the wine list.
Qǐng bǎ jiǔshuǐ dān gěi wǒ
请把酒水单给我。

877. May I have a look at the menu?
Qǐng gěi wǒ kàn kàn càipǔ
请给我看看菜谱.

878. What's the specialty of this restaurant?
Zhè ge cānguǎnde zhāopái cài shì shénme
这个餐馆的招牌菜是什么？

879. What do you recommend?
Yǒu shěnme cài kěyǐ tuījiàn yíxià ma
有什么菜可以推荐一下吗？

880. What would you like to have?
Nǐ xiǎng yào xiē shénme 你想要些什么？

881. Whatever you think of is fine with me.
Wǒ suí nǐ 我随你。

882. It's up to you.
Yíqiè yóu nǐ juédìng 一切由你决定。

883. I feel like having some noodles.
Wǒ hěn xiǎng chī miàn 我很想吃面。

884. I'd like something spicy.

Wǒ xiǎng chī xiē làde dōngxi 我想吃些辣的东西。

MORE: Tastes
Salty: xián 咸
Sour: suān 酸
Sweet: tián 甜
Bitter: kǔ 苦
Spicy: là 辣
If you put together sour-sweet-bitter-spicy, suān tián kǔ là 酸甜苦辣, it becomes a 4 character idiom which means the joys and sorrows of life.

885. Can I have the same dish as that?
Wǒ kěyǐ diǎn yǔ nà fèn xiāngtóngde cān ma
我可以点与那份相同的餐吗？

- Fèn 份 is a measure word for something to share or portions.

886. Do you have any vegetarian dishes?
Cāntīng shìfǒu yǒu gòngyīng sùshí cān
餐厅是否有供应素食餐？

887. The Beijing Duck sounds good to me.
Tīng qǐlai Běijīng Kǎoyā búcuò 听起来北京烤鸭不错。

- Qǐlai 起来 is used as a complement after a verb indicating impressions.

MORE: Chinese Dishes
Steamed Soup-dumplings: xiǎolóng bāo 小龙包
Dimsum: diǎnxīn 点心 (this also means snacks.
Since this is a Cantonese food, it usually is said in its Cantonese sound as dimsum.)
Hot and Sour Soup: suānlà tāng 酸辣汤
Kung Bao Chicken: gōngbǎo jīdīng 宫保鸡丁
Twice Cooked Pork; huíguō ròu 回鍋肉
Mapo Dofu: mápó dòufu 麻婆豆腐
Sweetened Vinegar Spareribs: táng cù páigǔ 糖醋排骨

888. What's your favorite food?

Nǐ zuì xǐhuan chī shénme 你最喜欢吃什么?

MORE: Western Dishes
Bread: miànbāo 面包
Ham: huǒtuǐ 火腿
Cheese: nǎilào 奶酪
Steak: niúpái 牛排
Hamburger: hànbǎo 汉堡
Hotdog: règǒu 热狗
Salad: shālā 沙拉
Sandwich: sānmíngzhì 三明治
Spagetti: Yìdàlì miàn 意大利面
Pizza: bǐsà 比萨
Fried Chicken: zhàjī 炸鸡

889. Waiter (waitress), I am ready to order.

Fúwù yuán, wǒ kěyǐ diǎn cài le 服务员, 我可以点菜了。

890. Can I take your order?

Nín yào diǎn cài ma 您要点菜吗?

891. We haven't decided yet.

Wǒmen hái méi juédìng 我们还没决定。

892. Please use less salt on my dishes.

Wǒ diǎnde cài qǐng shǎo fàng xiē yán
我点的菜请少放些盐。

893. Enjoy your meal.

Qǐng mànmànr xiǎngyòng ba 请慢慢儿享用吧。

894. Help yourself, please.

Qǐng zìjǐ yòng 请自己用。

895. Do you mind if I smoke?
Ní jièyì wǒ chōuyān ma
你介意我抽烟吗？

🎧896. Be my guest.
Qǐng biàn 请便。

897. I am going outside for a cigarette.
Wǒ qù wàimian chōu yì zhī yān 我去外面抽一支烟。
- Zhī 支 is a measure word for stick-like things.

🎧898. Cheers!
Gānbēi 干杯!

899. Bottoms up!
Gānbēi jiàn dǐ 干杯见底!

🎧900. As one pleases.
Suíyì 随意。
- This is used when you make a toast but don't want to bottoms up. It literally means you can drink as much or as less as you want.

🎧901. Cheers to our friendship!
Wèi wǒmende yǒuyí gānbēi 为我们的友谊干杯。
- Wèi………gānbēi 为………干杯 is used to specify the object of cheers.

🎧902. I can't drink.
Wǒ bú huì hē jiǔ 我不会喝酒。

🎧903. Let's drink our fill tonight.
Jìnwǎn wǒmen hē ge tòngkuai ba
今晚我们喝个痛快吧。

- Ge 个 is a measure word used between a verb and its complement.

904. I'll drink until I get drunk tonight!!
Jìntiān wǒ bú zuì bù xiū 今天我不醉不休。
- Bù 不……. bù 不 are used together when the first 不 is the condition of the second 不.

905. You have had too much.
Nǐ hē zuì le 你喝醉了。

906. Why don't you take a rest?
Zǎo diǎnr xiūxi ba 早点儿休息吧。

907. You think I am a drunkard?
Nǐ yǐwéi wǒ shì jiǔguǐ ya 你以为我是酒鬼呀？

 MORE: Drinks 2
The most popular alcoholic beverages in China are rice wine and beer. It may be a good idea to go with the toast suíyì 随意, since many Chinese rice wines are made from grains and herbs, and distilled to a high concentration, up to 50 ~ 60%!!
Gaoliang: gāoliáng jiǔ 高粱酒
Zhuyeqing: zhúyèqīng jiǔ 竹叶青酒
Maotai: máotái jiǔ 茅台酒 (máotái 茅台 is a place name in Guizhou province.)
Beer: píjiǔ 啤酒
Wine: pútáojiǔ 葡萄酒
Red wine: hóngjiǔ 红酒
White wine: báijiǔ 白酒
Brandy: báilándì 白兰地
Whisky: wèishìjiǔ 畏士酒
Champaign: xiāngbīnjiǔ 香槟酒
Cocktail: jīwěijiǔ 鸡尾酒

🎧908. I have a hangover.
Zuótiānde jiǔ hái méi xǐng ne 昨天的酒还没醒呢。

909. How often do you eat out?
Nǐ gé duōjiǔ zài wàimian chī yí cì fàn
你隔多久在外面吃一次饭？
- Gé 隔 is a verb meaning at an interval of.

910. Almost every other day.
Jīhu gé yì tiān 几乎隔一天。

🎧911. My mouth is watering.
Wǒ yào liú kǒushuǐ le 我要流口水了。

🎧912. It smells good.
Wén qǐlai hěn xiāng 闻起来很香。

913. This fish is fresh.
Zhè tiáo yú hěn xīnxiān 这条鱼很新鲜。
- Tiáo 条 is a measure word for something thin and long.

914. I picked out fish bones.
Wǒ bǎ yúgǔ dōu tiāo chūlái le 我把鱼骨都挑出來了。
- Chūlái 出來 is used after a verb to indicate outward movement.

🎧915. Are you used to the food here?
Nǐ xíguàn chī zhèrde fàncài ma
你习惯吃这儿的饭菜吗？

916. You'll get used to it.
Nǐ huì xíguàn de 你会习惯的。
- Huì 会 means be likely to.

917. This soup tastes great.

Zhè ge tāng fēicháng měiwèi 这个汤非常美味。

918. Do you like Chinese food?

Nǐ xǐhuan chī zhōngguó cài ma 你喜欢吃中国菜吗?

> **MORE: cài 菜**
> Adding cài 菜 after the name of a country makes that country's dish or cuisine. Cài 菜 is also used in Chinese regional cuisine names.
> Italian food: Yìdàlì cài 意大利菜
> French food: Fǎguó cài 法国菜
> Japanese food: Rìběn cài 日本菜
> Sichuan cuisine: Sìchuān cài 四川菜
> Cantonese cuisine: Guǎngdōng cài 广东菜

919. Is it delicious?

Hǎo bu hǎochī 好不好吃?

920. I'm on a diet.

Wǒ zài jiéshí 我在节食。

- Zài 在 means be, exist, and is a verb, but in this phrase it is used as a adverb to indicate an action in progress.

> **MORE: Zài 在**
> If you remember, we said there are no tenses in Chinese, and you might be wondering why a phrase like wǒ zài jiéshí 我在节食 is not considered as the present progressive form grammatically. This is because zài 在 is only indicating an action that is "in progress". Let's compare the below two sentences.
> I am on a diet. Wǒ zài jiéshí 我在节食.
> I was on a diet at that time. Nà shíhou, wǒ zài jiéshí 那时候, 我在节食.
> The second sentece was translated as a past sentence, because of the word nà shíhou 那时候, meaning at that time.

🎧921. I have to avoid food containing fat (salt/suger).
Wǒ bìxū bìmiǎn hán yóuzhī (yánfèn/ tángfèn) de shíwù
我必须避免含油脂(盐份/糖份)的食物。

🎧922. Please have some more.
Qǐng nǐ duō chī yìdiǎnr 请你多吃一点儿。

🎧923. I'm full.
Wǒ bǎo le 我饱了。

- If you look closely at the characters è 饿 and bǎo 饱, you will find the left side of both characters are the same 饣. The radical 饣 is a simplified radical of 食, which is from the character 食. 食 means to eat, food, or meal. Many food related terms carry the 食 radical.

924. I've had enough.
Wǒ yǐjīng chībǎo le 我已经吃饱了。

925. I'm full. I can't eat any more.
Wǒ bǎo le, bù néng zài chī le 我饱了，不能再吃了。

926. Thanks for the wonderful dinner.
Xièxiè nín fēngshèngde wǎncān
谢谢您丰盛的晚餐。

🎧927. Thank you for your hospitality.
Xièxiè nínde kuǎndài 谢谢您的款待。

🎧928. Thank you. I enjoyed it very much.
Xièxiè, wǒ zhēn shì tài gāoxìng le
谢谢，我真是太高兴了。

929. I'm glad you enjoyed it.
Nǐ xǐhuān wǒ jiù gāoxìng 你喜欢我就高兴。

- Jiù 就 connects two clauses, the first being the premise of the second.

930. I'll pick up the tab.
Wǒ lái fù zhàng 我来付帐。
- Lái 来 is used before a verb to indicate that one is about to do something.

931. The bill (check), please.
Láojià, jié zhàng 劳驾，结账。

932. Could I have the bill, please?
Qǐng bǎ zhàngdān gěi wǒ hǎo ma 请把账单给我好吗？

933. May I have a receipt?
Wǒ kěyǐ yào yì zhāng shōujù ma
我可以要一张收据吗？

934. Keep the change.
Búyòng zhǎo le 不用找了。

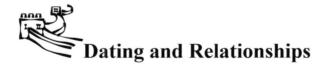 **Dating and Relationships**

935. I love you!
Wǒ ài nǐ 我爱你!

936. I love you too.
Wǒ yě ài nǐ 我也爱你。

937. You make me happy.
Nǐ shǐ wǒ gǎndào xìngfú 你使我感到幸福。

938. You do too.
Nǐ yě shǐ 你也是。

🎧939. I'm happy to have known you.
Néng rènshi nǐ wǒ fēicháng xìngfú
能认识你我非常幸福。

940. I can't help it.
Wǒ qíng bù zì jìn 我情不自禁。

941. It was love at first sight.
Wǒ shì yí jiàn zhōng qíng 我是一见钟情。

🎧942. You're my type.
Nǐ shì wǒ xǐhuande nà zhǒng lèixíng
你是我喜欢的那种类型。

🎧943. You have beautiful eyes.
Nǐde yǎnjīng zhēn měi 你的眼睛真美。

944. You're sweet/ beautiful/ sexy.
Nǐ zhēn hǎo/ piàoliang/ xìnggǎn 你真好/ 漂亮/ 性感 。

945. You're the most beautiful woman I've ever seen.
Nǐ shì wǒ jiàndào guo de zuì měide nǚrén
你是我见到过的最美的女人。

946. I'm crazy for you.
Nǐ shǐ wǒ fāfēng 你使我发疯。

🎧947. Tell me everything about yourself.
Qǐng gàosù wǒ yǒu guān nǐde yíqiè
请告诉我有关你的一切。

🎧948. We have a lot in common.
Wǒmen yǒu hěn duō xiāngtóng zhī chù
我们有很多相同之处。

949. I want you to meet my parents.
Wǒ xiǎng ràng nǐ jiàn jiàn wǒde fùmǔ
我想让你见见我的父母。

950. I can't handle a girl like her.
Wǒ bù gǎn dǎ xiàng tā nà yàngde gūniangde zhǔyi
我不敢打像她那样的姑娘的主意。
  • Dǎ zhǔyi 打主意 means try to obtain.

🎧951. I'm dying to see her.
Wǒ fēicháng xiǎng jiàndào tā 我非常想见到她。

952. I am crazy about her.
Wǒ duì tā zháomí le 我对她着迷了。

🎧953. I want to pursue her.
Wǒ xiǎng zhuīqiú tā 我想追求她。

954. I'm trying to pick her up.
Wǒ dǎsuan bǎ tā nòng dàoshǒu 我打算把她弄到手。

955. I'm trying to get a date with her.
Wǒ dǎsuan hé tā yuēhuì 我打算和她约会。

956. Can I see you again?
Wǒmen hái kěyǐ zài jiànmiàn ma 我们还可以再见面吗?

🎧957. Can I have your phone number?
Nǐ néng gěi wǒ nǐde diànhuà hàomǎ ma
你能给我你的电话号码吗?

🎧958. Are you free tonight?
Jīnwǎn yǒu kòng ma 今晚有空吗？

959. Yes. Why?
Yǒu kòng, gànmá 有空，干嘛？

960. Do you have plans tonight?
Jīntiān wǎnshang yǒu shì ma 今天晚上有事吗？

961. Do you want to go out with me tonight?
Jīnwǎn nǐ néng hé wǒ yuēhuì ma
今晚你能和我约会吗？

🎧962. Let's go out tonight.
Jīnwǎn chūqù ba 今晚出去吧。

963. If you're free, why don't we go out tonight?
Yàoshì wǎnshang yǒu kòng, wǒmen chūqù zǒu zǒu xíng ma
要是晚上有空，我们出去走走行吗？

964. Could you keep me company for a while?
Néng péi péi wǒ ma 能陪陪我吗？

965. Would you like to go to a movie with me?
Nǐ yuànyì hé wǒ yìqǐ qù kàn diànyǐng ma
你愿意和我一起去看电影吗？

🎧966. Would you like to go to a show?
Nǐ xiǎng qù kàn yǎnchū ma
你想去看演出吗？

🎧967. Sure, I'd love to.
Dāngrán, wǒ hěn xiǎng qù 当然，我很想去。

968. Sorry, I have a boyfriend.
Duìbuqǐ, wǒ yǒu nán péngyou le
对不起，我有男朋友了。

969. He broke up with his girlfriend.
Tā gēn tāde nǚ péngyou chuī le 他跟他的女朋友吹了。

970. Look! You lost your mind after seeing a
pretty woman!
Nǐ a, jiànle piàoliangde nǚrén,
lián húnr dōu méi le
你啊，见了漂亮的女人，连魂儿都没了！

- A 啊 is used before a pause in order to attract attention.

971. Where do you want to meet?
Zài nǎr jiànmiàn 在哪儿见面？

972. Any place you want.
Nǐ juéde nǎr héshì jiù zài nǎr
你觉得哪儿合适就在哪儿。

973. What time should we meet?
Wǒmen jǐ diǎn jiànmiàn 我们几点见面？

974. How about seven?
Qī diǎn zěnme yàng 7点怎么样？

975. Do you want me to pick you up?
Yào wǒ kāi chē qù jiē nǐ ma 要我开车去接你吗？

976. Let's walk hand in hand.
Wǒmen lāzhe shǒu zǒu ba
我们拉着手走吧。

🎧977. May I hold your hand?

Wǒ kěyǐ qiān nǐ de shǒu ma 我可以牵你的手吗?

978. Your hand feels cold.

Nǐde shǒu mō qǐlai hěn lěng 你的手摸起来很冷。

979. Here, wear my jacket.

Gěi, chuānshàng wǒde jiākè ba 给，穿上我的夹克吧。

- Shàng 上 is used after a verb to indicate achievement of one's goal.

🎧980. I'll miss you.

Wǒ huì xiǎng nǐ de 我会想你的。

981. I'll miss you, too.

Wǒ yě huì xiǎng nǐ de 我也会想你的。

🎧982. I wish I could be with you.

Wǒ zhēn xīwàng néng hé nǐ zài yìqǐ
我真希望能和你在一起。

983. So do I.

Wǒ yě shì 我也是。

🎧984. Here's a gift for you.

Zhèli yǒu ge lǐwù sòng gěi nǐ 这里有个礼物送给你。

985. Open the box.

Nǐ dǎkāi hézi kàn kàn 你打开盒子看看。

🎧986. He doesn't care about me.

Tā bìng bú zàihu wǒ 他并不在乎我。

- Bìng 并 means at all or not at all, is used before a negative for emphasis.

🎧987. Love can not be forced.
Gǎnqíng shì bù néng miǎnqiáng de 感情是不能勉强的。

988. She wouldn't even talk to me.
Tā lián huà dōu bù gēn wǒ shuō
她连话都不跟我说。

- Lián 连 means even and is usually used with dōu 都.

🎧989. I don't want to get serious yet.
Wǒ hái bù xiǎng tài rènzhēn 我还不想太认真。

990. I just want to have fun.
Wǒ xiànzàizhǐshì xiàng wánr wánr
我现在只是想玩儿玩儿。

991. I didn't know you felt that way.
Wǒ yìdiǎnr dōu bù zhīdào nǐde gǎnjué
我一点儿都不知道你的感觉。

🎧992. Why do you like me?
Wǒ wèi shénme xǐhuān wǒ 你为什么喜欢我?

993. Love doesn't have national boundaries.
Àiqíng bù fēn guójiè 爱情不分国界 。

🎧994. You are so heartless.
Nǐ yě tài hěnxīn le 你也太狠心了。

995. You broke my heart.
Nǐ shāng le wǒde xīn 你伤了我的心。

🎧996. I didn't mean to...
Wǒ bú shì nà ge yìsi 我不是那个意思……

997. I wish I had never met you.
Wǒ zhēn xīwàng cónglái dōu méi yùdàoguo nǐ
我真希望我从来都没遇到过你。

- When cónglái 从来 comes in a negative sentence, it means ever. Dào 到 comes after a verb as a complement to indicate success. Guo 过 is indicating completion of an action as an experience.

998. I regret meeting you.
Wǒ zhēn hòuhuǐ rènshile nǐ 我真后悔认识了你。

999. He is single.
Tā shì dānshēn guìzú 他是单身贵族。

1000. They adore each other.
Tāmen hùxiāng qīngmù 他们互相倾慕。

1001. He is a good-looking guy.
Tā shì ge měi nánzi 他是个美男子。

1002. He dates around a lot.
Tā hé hǎo dūo nǔrén láiwǎng 他和好多女人来往。

1003. He is a real playboy.
Tā zhēn shì ge huā huā gōngzi 他真是个花花公子。

- Huā huā gōngzi 花花公子 is a magazine's name as well.

1004. He really turns me on.
Tā zhēn ràng wǒ shénhún diāndǎo 他真让我神魂颠倒。

1005. He breaks a lot of hearts.
Tā shǐ hěn duō nǔrén chángdàole shīliànde tòngkǔ
他使很多女人尝到了失恋的痛苦。

1006. She is a knockout.

Tā zhēn mírén ya 她真迷人呀。

🎧1007. I think he has a crush on you.
Tā hǎoxiàng kànshang nǐ le 他好像看上你了。
- Shang 上 is used after a verb to indicate the beginning and the contunity of an action.

1008. She seems to like me.
Tā hǎoxiàng xǐhuānshang wǒ le 她好像喜欢上我了。

1009. She has been coming on to me.
Tā duì wǒ yǒu yìsi 她对我有意思。

🎧1010. Don't put on a pose.
Bié zhuāngqiāng zuòshì 别装腔作势。

1011. She's just playing hard to get.
Tā zhǐ shì zài diào nǐde wèikǒu 她只是在吊你的胃口。
- Wèikǒu 胃口 means appetite and liking.

🎧1012. When are you getting married?
Nǐ shénme shíhou jiéhūn 你什么时候结婚?

1013. I want to get married, but……
Wǒ xiǎng jiéhūn, dànshì…… 我想结婚, 但是……

🎧1014. They got married after she got pregnant.
Tāmen shì xiān shàng chē hòu bǔ piào de
他们是先上车后补票的。
- Literally this means they bought tickets after getting on the bus.

1015. They got married after getting pregnant.
Fēng zǐ chéng mìng 奉子成命。
- Literally means fulfilled the child's order.

 **Medical**

🎧1016. I have a cold.
Wǒ gǎnmào le 我感冒了。

1017. I have a slight cold.
Wǒ yǒudiǎnr gǎnmào
我有点儿感冒。

1018. I have a bad cold
Wǒ déle zhòng gǎnmào
我得了重感冒。

- Dé 得 is a verb meaning get or obtain.

🎧1019. I feel chilly.
Wǒ húnshēn fā lěng 我浑身发冷。

1020. I've got a runny nose.
Wǒ liú bí shuǐ 我流鼻水。

🎧1021. I have a sore throat.
Wǒ hóulóng tòng 我喉咙痛。

🎧1022. I've been coughing day and night.
Wǒ zǎowǎn dōu zài késou 我早晚都在咳嗽。

🎧1023. I can't stop sneezing.
Wǒ dǎ pēntì dǎ ge bù tíng
我打喷嚏打个不停。

- Please look at the left side of the words hóulóng 喉咙 (throat), késou 咳嗽(cough) and pēntì 喷嚏 (sneeze). All of their radicals are 口，which means mouth. Ge 个 is used between a verb (打) and its compliment (不停).

1024. I've got a temperature.
Wǒ fāshāo le 我发烧了。

1025. I'm running a high fever.
Wǒ fā gāo shāo 我发高烧。

1026. Be careful not to catch a cold
Xiǎoxīn bú yào dé gǎnmào 小心不要得感冒。

1027. I felt sort of ill.
Wǒ gǎnjué yǒudiǎnr búshì 我感觉有点儿不适。

1028. I'm not feeling well
Wǒ juéde shēnti bù shūfu 我觉得身体不舒服。

1029. I'm not quite myself.
Wǒ yǒudiǎnr bù duìjìnr 我有点儿不对劲儿。

1030. I sprained my ankle/back.
Wǒ niǔ le huái/ yāo 我扭了踝/腰。

1031. Do you want to try acupuncture?
Xiǎng bu xiǎng shì yí xià zhēnjiǔ
想不想试一下针灸？

1032. Is acupuncture safe?
Zhēnjiǔ ān bu ānquán 针灸安不安全？

1033. I broke my leg.
Wǒ bǎ tuǐ shuāiduàn le 我把腿摔断了。

1034. What's your trouble?
Nǐ nǎr bù shūfu 你哪儿不舒服?

🎧1035. My cut hurts.
Shāngkǒu téng 伤口疼。

1036. Do you need a doctor?
Jiào yīshēng ma 叫医生吗?

1037. Yes, I think so.
Shìde, qǐng jiào yīshēng ba 是的，请叫医生吧。
- Nurse is called hùshì 护士.

1038. Do you want to see a Western doctor or Oriental doctor?
Nǐ yào kàn xīyī háishì kàn zhōngyī
你要看西医还是看中医?

🎧1039. Could you send me a doctor?
Nǐ néng bāng wǒ qǐng wèi yīshēng ma
你能帮我请位医生吗?
- Wèi 位 is a measure word for a person in a polite way.

1040. Do you need any help?
Xūyào bāngmáng ma 需要帮忙吗?

1041. Please call an ambulance.
Qǐng jiào jiùhù chē 请叫救护车。
- Emergency Room: jíjiù zhàn 急救站
- Emergency treatment: jízhěn 急诊

🎧1042. I'd like to see a doctor.
Wǒ yào kànbìng 我要看病。

🎧1043. What's wrong with you?
Nǐ zěnme la 你怎么啦?

🎧1044. What are your symptoms?
Shì shénme zhèngzhuàng 是什么症状?

1045. Let me check your temperature.
Liáng yíxià tǐwēn ba 量一下体温吧。

1046. I'd like to check check your blood pressure.
Wǒ liáng yi liáng nǐde xuěyā
我量一量你的血压。

🎧1047. I have high/low blood pressure.
Wǒde xuěyā gāo/dī 我的血压高/低。

> **MORE: Blood**
> Blood Test: huàyàn xuě 化验血
> Take blood: chōu xuě 抽血
> Blood type: xuěxíng 血型

1048. Is that so?
Shì ma 是吗?

🎧1049. What's wrong with me?
Wǒ nǎr bù hǎo 我哪儿不好?

1050. Is it serious?
Yǎnzhòng ma 严重吗?

🎧1051. Do I need surgery?
Wǒ xūyào dòng shǒushù 我需要动手术吗?
   •   Another common term for surgery is kāidāo 开刀.

1052. Are you taking any medication?
Nǐ cháng fúyòng shénme yào 你常服用什么药？

🎧1053. I'm not taking any medication.
Wǒ méi fúyòng rènhé yào 我没服用任何药。

1054. I'll give you a prescription.
Wǒ huì gěi nǐ kāi ge chǔfáng
我会给你开个处方。

1055. Please pick up your medication at the
pharmacy.
Qǐng dào yàofáng ná nǐde yào
请到药房拿你的药。

1056. Please take your medication as directed.
Qǐng ànzhào yīshēngde zhǐshì fúyào
请按照医生的指示服药。

🎧1057. Please take your medication on time.
Qǐng ànshí fúyào 请按时服药。

1058. To be taken three times a day, two tablets each time.
Rì fú sān cì, měi cì liǎng piàn 日服三次，每次两片。
• Piàn 片 is a measure word for things in slices.

🎧1059. Aren't you feeling well?
Nǐ bù shūfu ma 你不舒服吗？

1060. No, I'm just tired.
Méiyǒu, zhǐshì yǒudiǎnr lèi 没有，只是有点儿累。

🎧1061. I am a little better today.
Wǒ jīntiān hǎo yìdiǎnr le 我今天好一点儿了。

🎧1062. Did you sleep alright?

Shuìde hǎo ma 睡得好吗?

1063. Yes, I slept very well.

Ng, shuìde tǐng hǎo 嗯，睡得挺好。

- Ng 嗯 is an interjection indicating response.

🎧1064. No, I couldn't fall asleep.

Nǎr a, jīhū méi shuì zháo 哪儿啊，几乎没睡着。

- Zháo 着 is used after a verb to indicate result.

 MORE: Medical Terms

Outpatient department: ménzhěn bù 门诊部

Clinic: zhěnliáo suǒ 诊疗所

Clinic: wèishēng shì 卫生室

Making appointment: yùyuē 预约

Register: guàhào 挂号

Registration card: guàhào zhèng 挂号证

Be hospitalized: zhùyuàn 住院

Be discharged: chūyuàn 出院

Treatment method: zhìliáo fāngfǎ 治疗方法

Give an injection: dǎzhēn 打针

Recuperate: yǎngbìng 养病

Traffic accident: chēhuò 车祸

Cancer: áizhèng 癌症

AIDS: āizī bìng 艾滋病

Heart disease: xīnzàng bìng 心脏病

Pharmacy：yàodiàn 药店

Surgery: wàikē 外科

Internal Medicine: nèikē 内科

Pediatrics: érkē 儿科

OB GYN: fùchǎnkē 妇产科

Orthopedics: gǔkē 骨科

Dental clinic: yákē 牙科

Dermatology: pífūkē 皮肤科

Otolaryngology: ěrbíhóukē 耳鼻喉科

1065. You look pale.
Nǐde liǎnsè hěn nánkàn 你的脸色很难看。

🎧1066. Are you okay?
Méishì ba 没事吧?

🎧1067. I guess I'm just tired.
Wǒ xiǎng kěnéng shì yǒudiǎnr lèi le
我想可能是有点儿累了。

1068. You don't look well.
Nǐ kàn shàngqu shēntǐ bú tài hǎo
你看上去身体不太好。

🎧1069. I feel bad.
Wǒ juéde nánshòu 我觉得难受。

1070. Please sit down for a while.
Nǐ zuò huìr ba 你坐会儿吧。

🎧1071. I have a stomachache.
Wǒ dùzi téng 我肚子疼。

1072. How long have you had it?
Téng duō cháng shíjiān le 疼多长时间了?

1073. Did you eat too much?
Shì búshì chī duō le 是不是吃多了?

🎧1074. Did you eat something unusual?
Chī le shénme bú duìjìnrde dōngxi méiyǒu
吃了什么不对劲的东西没有?

- Méiyǒu 没有 is a adverb used to form the negation of a completed action.

1075. I have diarrhea.

Wǒ lā dùzi le 我拉肚子了。

🎧1076. I have food poisoning.

Wǒ shíwù zhòngdú le 我食物中毒了。

🎧1077. I have a dull pain.

Wǒ gǎndào yǐnyǐn zuòtòng 我感到隐隐作痛。

1078. I have a sharp pain.

Wǒ gǎndào zuānxīnde téng 我感到钻心地疼。

- De 地 is used after an adjective, a noun, or a phrase to form an adverbial adjunct before the verb.

1079. I have a throbbing pain

Wǒ gǎndào yí tiào yí tiàode téng

我感到一跳一跳地疼。

1080. I have terrible pain.

Wǒ gǎndào jù tòng 我感到巨痛。

🎧1081. I have a piercing pain.

Wǒ gǎndào cìgǔde téng 我感到刺骨地疼。

1082. I have a stabbing pain

Wǒ gǎndào xiàng zhēn zhā sìde téng

我感到像针扎似地疼。.

- Xiàng 像 and sìde 似地 are usually used together meaning, like or as if.

🎧1083. I have a headache.

Wǒ tóu téng 我头疼。

1084. I have a splitting headache.

Wǒde tóu xiàng lièle sìde téng
我的头像裂了似地疼。

1085. I've got a very bad headache.
Wǒ tóu hěn tòng 我头很痛。

1086. This headache is killing me.
Wǒ tóu kuài tòng sǐ le 我头快痛死了。
   • Sǐ 死 means die, dead, and extremely as an adverb.

1087. I need some pain killer.
Wǒ yào yì xiē zhèntòng piàn 我要一些镇痛片。

1088. My head is swimming.
Wǒ tóuhūn nǎo zhàng 我头昏脑胀的。
   • Literally means head is dizzy and brain is expanding.

1089. I have a toothache.
Wǒ yá téng 我牙疼。

1090. My tooth is killing me.
Wǒde yá téng sǐ le 我的牙疼死了。

1091. When did it start?
Shénme shíhou kāishǐ de 什么时候开始的?

1092. I feel dizzy.
Wǒ tóu yùn mù xuán 我头晕目眩。

1093. I feel sluggish.
Wǒ hún shēn méijìnr 我浑身没劲儿。

1094. I don't have any appetite.

Wǒ méiyǒu shíyù 我没有食欲。

🎧1095. I don't have much of an appetite these days.
Zuìjìn wǒ méi shénme shíyù 最近我没什么食欲。

1096. You should eat something.
Nà nǐ yě děi chī diǎnr dōngxi 那你也得吃点儿东西。
- Nà 那 in this sentence is a conjunction meaning in that case.

🎧1097. I feel sore and ache all over.
Wǒ juéde quán shēn suān tòng
我觉得全身酸痛。

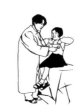

1098. I feel like I'm dying.
Wǒ juéde wǒ hǎoxiàng yào sǐ le yíyàng
我觉得我好象要死了一样。

1099. She suffered from a bad cold.
Tā huànle zhòng gǎnmào 她患了重感冒。

🎧1100. She passed out.
Tā hūn guòqù le 她昏过去了。
- Guòqù 过去 is used after a verb to indicate loss of consciousness.

🎧1101. He is ill in bed.
Tā wò bìng zài chuáng
他卧病在床。

1102. Is he okay?
Tā hǎo ma 他好吗?

1103. He's getting better.
Hǎo duō le 好多了。

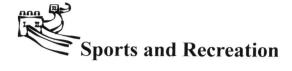

Sports and Recreation

🎧1104. I am a soccer fan.
Wǒ shì ge zúqiú mí 我是个足球迷。
- Zúqiú 足球 usually means soccer, and when needed to be verified, it's called yīngshì zúqiú 英式足球. American football is called měishì zúqiú 美式足球.

1105. I am going to a soccer game.
Wǒ qù kàn zúqiú sài 我去看足球赛。

1106. I love this game.
Wǒ zhōng'ài zhè xiàng yùndòng 我钟爱这项运动。
- Xiàng 项 is a measure word for item.

🎧1107. Which teams are playing?
Shéi gēn shéi bǐsài 谁跟谁比赛?

1108. Who's kicking off?
Xiànzài shì shéi zài kāiqiú 现在是谁在开球?

🎧1109. Who won the game?
Shéi yíng le 谁赢了?

1110. Which team lost the game?
Nǎ ge duì shū le 哪个队输了?

🎧1111. They scored a point at first half.
Zài qián bàn cháng tāmen jìnle yí ge qiú
在前半场他们进了一个球。

1112. What's the score?
Jǐ bǐ Jǐ 几比几?

1113. They played very well.
Tāmen tīde hěn hǎo 他们踢得很好。

1114. The referee said that the goal wasn't countable.
Cáipàn shuō nà ge qiú bú suàn
裁判说那个球不算。

1115. I think the referee isn't fair.
Wǒ juéde cáipàn bù gōngpíng
我觉得裁判不公平。

1116. What kind of sports do you like to play?
Nǐ xǐhuan shénme yùndòng 你喜欢什么运动?

1117. I like both hiking and swimmimg.
Páshān hé yóuyǒng wǒ dōu xǐhuan
爬山和游泳我都喜欢。

1118. I like to play tennis, and I often play table tennis too.
Wǒ xǐhuan dǎ wǎngqiú, yě chángcháng dǎ pīngpāng qiú
我喜欢打网球, 也常常打乒乓球。

 MORE: Ball Games
Volley ball: páiqíu 排球
Badminton: yúmáoqíu 羽毛球
Baseball: bàngqíu 棒球
Softball: lěiqíu 垒球
Handball: shǒuqíu 手球
Hockey: qūgùnqíu 曲棍球
Ice Hockey: bīngqíu 冰球
Golf: gāoěrfūqíu 高尔夫球

🎧1119. How is your swimmimg?
Nǐ yóuyǒng yóude hǎo bu hǎo
你游泳游得好不好？

1120. It's OK.
Hái kěyǐ 还可以。

1121. I am not as good as you are.
Méiyǒu nǐ yóude nàme hǎo 没有游得你那么好。

MORE: Swimming
Swimming pool: yóuyǒng chí 游泳池
Changing room: gēngyīshì 更衣室
Shower: línyù 淋浴
Diving platform:tiàotái 跳台
Swimming trunks : yǒngkù 泳裤
Swimming suit : yǒngyī 泳衣
Swimming cap: yǒngmào 泳帽

🎧1122. What time do you want to go bowling?
Nǐ xiǎng shénme shíhou qù dǎ bǎolíng qíu
你想什么时候去打保龄球呀？
- Bǎolíng 保龄 is a transliteration of bowling.

1123. Do you know how to play basket ball?
Nǐ huì dǎ lánqiú ma 你会打篮球吗？

🎧1124. Skating is interesting.
Huábīng hěn yǒuqù 滑冰很有趣。

1125. I'm going skiing.
Wǒ yào qù huáxué 我要去滑雪。

🎧1126. Just for entertainment.
Zhǐshì wèile xiāoqiǎn yíxià 只是为了消遣一下。

🎧1127. Where can I buy a ticket?
Zài nǎr mǎi piào 在哪儿买票?

1128. At that counter.
Zài nà ge guìtái 在那个柜台。

1129. Let's stand in the line.
Wǒmen xiān páiduì ba 我们先排队吧。

🎧1130. Don't cut in line.
Bú yào chā duì 不要插队。

🎧1131. I'd like two adults tickets for 7 o'clock.
Wǒ yào liǎng zhāng qī diǎnde chéngrén piào
我要两张七点的成人票。

- Zhāng 张 is a measure word for something flat, such as paper.

🎧1132. Do you have any tickets for the game?
Háiyou nà chǎng bǐsàide piào ma
还有那场比赛的票吗?

- Chǎng 场 is a measure word for sports and recreation.

1133. Sorry, we're sold out.
Duìbuqǐ, mài wán le 对不起, 卖完了。

1134. Can I make a reservation?
Kěyǐ yùdìng ma 可以预订吗?

🎧1135. I'd like two tickets for Mar 5th, please.
Wǒ mǎi liǎng zhāng sān yuè wǔ hàode piào
我买两张 3 月 5 号的票。

🎧1136. What time does it start?

Jǐ diǎn kāishǐ 几点开始?

1137. What movie is on tonight?
Jīntiān wǎnshang fàng shénme diànyǐng
今天晚上放什么电影?

1138. What movie do you want to see?
Nǐ xiǎng kàn shénme diànyǐng
你想看什么电影?

🎧1139. Who is in this movie?
Zhè bù diànyǐng shì shéi yǎn de 这部电影是谁演的?
   • Bù 部 is a measure word for film or work.

1140. I'm his fan.
Wǒ shì tāde yǐngmí 我是他的影迷。

1141. How long does it last?
Yǎn duōcháng shíjiān 演多长时间?

🎧1142. What time is the next showing?
Xià yì chǎng jǐ diǎn kāiyǎn 下一场几点开演?

1143. What time will it be over?
Jǐ diǎn yǎn wán 几点演完?

🎧1144. Is this seat taken?
Zhè wèizi yǒu rén ma 这位子有人吗?

1145. No, it's not.
Bù, méi rén 不，没人。

🎧1146. We have great seats, don't we?
Wǒmen zhè ge wèizi zhēn bàng 我们这个位子真棒。

1147. That person is blocking my view.
Qiánbiande rén dǎngzhe, wǒ kàn bú jiàn
前边的人挡着，我看不见。

1148. We are way in the back, aren't we?
Wǒmen zěnme zuòde zhème kào hòu ya
我们怎么坐得这么靠后呀?

1149. Let's sit closer up front.
Wǒmen zuòdào qiánmiande zuòwèishàng ba
我们坐到前面的座位上吧。

1150. That was interesting, wasn't it?
Zhēn tài yǒu yìsi le, shì búshì
真太有意思了，是不是?

1151. It sure was.
Quèshí 确实。

1152. I was moved.
Tài ràng rén gǎndòng le 太让人感动了。

1153. It was a touching movie.
Zhè shì yí bù gǎnrénde diànyǐng 这是一部感人的电影。

1154. That was boring, wasn't it?
Zhè diànyǐng zhēn méijìn 这电影真没劲。

1155. I almost dozed off.
Wǒ chādiǎn dǎ kēshuì le 我差点打瞌睡了。

 **Travel**

1156. Where can I check in?
Zài nǎr bànli dēngjì shǒuxù
在那儿办理登记手续？

1157. I'd like to make a reservation.
Wǒ xiǎng dìng piào 我想订票。

1158. This is China Civil Airlines 123, bound for Beijing.
Nín chéngzuòde shì Zhōngguó Mínháng kāiwǎng
Běijīngde yī èr sān hào bānjī
您乘坐的是中国民航开往北京的 123 号班机。

1159. Do you want coffee or tea?
Nǐ yào kāfēi háishì yào chá
你要咖啡还是要茶？

1160. Welcome to Beijing !
Huānyíng láidào Běijīng 欢迎来到北京!

1161. Did you enjoy your flight?
Nǐde fēixíng lǔtú yúkuài ma 你的飞行旅途愉快吗？

1162. What's your first impression of Beijing?
Běijīng gěi nǐde dì yí ge gǎnjué shì shénme
北京给你的第一个感觉是什么？

1163. How do you find Beijing?
Nǐ juéde Běijīng zěnme yàng
你觉得北京怎么样？

🎧1164. Beijing is a city full of energy.
Běijīng shì yí zuò chōngmǎn huólìde chéngshì
北京是一座充满活力的城市。

- Zuò 座 is a measure word for a large and solid thing.

1165. The people in Beijing are very friendly.
Běijīng rén fēicháng rèqíng 北京人非常热情。

🎧1166. How long have you lived in Beijing?
Nǐ zhù Běijīng zhùle duō jiǔ 你住北京住了 多久?

1167. I was born and raised in Beijing.
Wǒ shì Běijīng tǔshēng tǔzhǎng de 我是北京土生长的。

🎧1168. I want to reserve a room.
Wǒ xiǎng yùdìng yí ge fángjiān
我想预定一个房间。

1169. Do you have a room available?
Nǐmen yǒu kōng fángjiān ma 你们有空房间吗?

🎧1170. Have you got anything larger?
Yǒu dà yìdiǎnrde ma 有大一点儿的吗?

1171. How many days do you want to stay?
Nǐ yào zhù jǐ tiān 你要住几天?

1172. Can you give me a wake-up call?
Nǐ néng dǎ diànhuà jiàoxǐng wǒ ma
你能打电话叫醒我吗?

1173. We don't have any room available now. It's a full-house.
Xiànzài méiyǒu kōng fángjiān, dōu zhù mǎn le

现在没有空房间，都住满了。

1174. Could you recommend a nice restaurant near here?
Shìfǒu kě jièshào yì jiā fùjìn kǒubēi
búcuòde cāntīng
是否可介绍一家附近口碑不错的餐厅？
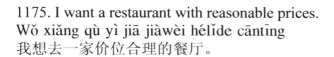
- Jiā 家 is a measure word used to count
  enterprises.

1175. I want a restaurant with reasonable prices.
Wǒ xiǎng qù yì jiā jiàwèi hélǐde cāntīng
我想去一家价位合理的餐厅。

1176. I'd like to try some local food.
Wǒ xiǎng chángshì yíxià dāngdì shíwù
我想尝试一下当地食物。

1177. The view is great.
Jǐngsè duōme piàoliang 景色多么漂亮!
- Duōme 多么 is a adverb used in an exclamatory sentence
  indicating high degree.

1178. Could you take a picture for me?
Qǐng nín bāng wǒ zhào yì zhāng
xiàng , hǎo ma
请您帮我照一张相， 好吗？

1179. Everyone stand closer, please.
Qǐng dàjiā zhànde jǐn yì diǎn 请大家站得紧一点。

1180. Excuse me, what's the exchange
rate for US dollar and RMB today?
Qǐngwèn, jīntiān měijīn duì rénmínbìde
huìlǜ duōshao
请问，今天美金对人民币的汇率多少？
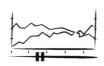

1181. What kind of currency do you want to change?
Nín yào huàn nǎ zhǒng huòbì 您要换哪种货币？

🎧1182. I'd like to change US $ 300.
Wǒ yào huàn měijīn sān bǎi kuài 我要换美金 300 块。

 MORE: Currency
HKD: Gǎngbì 港币
JPY: Rìyuán 日元
EUR: Ōuyuán 欧元
GBP: Yīngbàng 英镑
CAD: Jiānádàyuán 加拿大元
AUD: Àudàlìyǎyuán 澳大利亚元

🎧1183. Is it in traveler's check or in cash?
Nà shì lǚxíng zhīpiào háishì xiànjīn
那是旅行支票还是现金？

1184. How would you like it?
Nín yào shénme miàn'é de 您要什么面额的？

🎧1185. All in 10 yuan notes, please.
Quánbù shí yuánde hǎo le 全部 10 元的好了。

1186. Please count them.
Qǐng shǔ yi shǔ 请数一数。

1187. I've never been to Shanghai.
Wǒ méiyǒu qùguo Shànghǎi 我没有去过上海。

🎧1188. I want to visit Shanghai by train.
Wǒ xiǎng zuò huǒchē qù Shànghǎi
kànkàn
我想坐火车去上海看看。

1189. How far is it from Beijing to Shanghai?

Cóng Běijīng dào Shànghǎi yǒu duō yuǎn

从北京到上海有多远？

1190. It's 1463 km, about 909 miles.

Yǒu yī qiān sì bǎi liù shí sān gōnglǐ, děngyú jiǔ bǎi líng jiǔ yīnglǐ 有 1463 公里，等于 909 英里。

MORE: Measurement

Millimeter : háomǐ 毫米

Centimeter: límǐ 厘米

Meter : mǐ 米

Gram : kè 克

Kilogram : gōngjīn 公斤

Ton : gōngdùn 公顿

Foot : yīngchǐ 英尺

Inch : yīngcùn 英寸

Square meter: píngfāng mǐ 平方米

Hectare: gōngqǐng 公顷

Square kilometer : píngfāng gōnglǐ 平方公里

Milliter : háoshēng 毫升

Liter: shēng 升

Nautical mile: hǎilǐ 海里

Pound : bàng 磅

Watt: wǎtè 瓦特

Volt: fútè 伏特

1191. I want to buy 2 tickets to Shanghai by express.

Wǒ xiǎng mǎi liǎng zhāng qù Shànghǎide zhídá tèkuài piào

我想买两张去上海的直达特快票。

1192. Do you want a hard seat, soft seat, hard bed, or soft bed?

Nǐ yào yìngzuò, ruǎnzuò, yìngwò háishì ruǎnwò

你要硬座，软座，硬卧还是软卧？

1193. How much is a soft bed?
Ruǎnwò shì duōshao 软卧是多少？

1194. 500 RMB each.
Yì zhāng wǔ bǎi kuài 一张五百块。

1195. How long does it take from Beijing to Shanghai?
Cóng Běijīng dào Shànghǎi yào duōjiǔ
从北京到上海要多久？

1196. About 12 hours.
Dàyuē shí èr ge zhōngtóu 大约 12 个锺头。

1197. Did you have fun？
Nǐ wánde kāixīn ma 你玩得开心吗？

1198. I'm having fun.
Wǒ wánde hěn kāixīn 我玩得很开心。

1199. When are you off?
Nǐ shénme shíhou zǒu 你什么时候走？

1200. I'm flying back tomorrow.
Wǒ míngtiān zuò fēijī huíqù 我明天坐飞机回去。

1201. Could you drop me off at the airport?
Nǐ néng zài wǒ dào fēijīcháng ma
你能载我到飞机场吗？

1202. Are you coming with me?
Nǐ gēn wǒ yìqǐ qù ma 你跟我一起去吗？

🎧1203. Did you have a nice holiday?

Nǐ jiàqí guòde yúkuài ma 你假期过得愉快吗？

1204. I hope you will come back to Beijing again!

Xīwàng nǐ néng zài lái Běijīng zuòkè

希望你能再来北京做客!

1205. My cell phone is not working.

Wǒde shǒujī huài le 我的手机坏了。

- Mobile phone is also called yídòng diànhuà 移动电话.

1206. That payphone is out of order.

Nà ge gōngyòng diànhuà chū gùzhāng le

那个公用电话出故障了。

🎧1207. I couldn't get through.

Wǒ dǎ bu tōng diànhuà 我打不通电话。

🎧1208. I have a complaint.

Wǒ yào tóusù 我要投诉。

1209. Who is in charge here?

Zhèli shéi fùzé 这里谁负责?

🎧1210. I'd like a refund.

Wǒ xiǎng yào tuìkuǎn 我想要退款。

1211. I want to report a theft.

Wǒ yào bào yì zōng dàoqiè àn

我要报一宗盗窃案。

🎧1212. I had my camera stolen.

Wǒde zhàoxiàngjī gěi rén tōuzǒu le

我的照相机给人偷走了。

- Gěi 给 is a preposition used as a passive indicator.

1213. I lost my wallet and passport.
Wǒ diūle wǒde qiánbāo hé hùzhào
我丢了我的钱包和护照。

1214. That happens.
Zhèyàngde shìqíng jīngcháng fāshēng
这样的事情经常发生。

1215. These things happen all the time.
Zhè shì cháng yǒude shì 这是常有的事。

1216. I'll check it.
Wǒ qù chá yíxià 我去查一下。

1217. I am going to the Chinese embassy to get a visa.
Wǒ yào qù Zhōngguó dàshǐguǎn bàn qiānzhèng
我要去中国大使馆办签证。

1218. Would you do me a favor?
Nǐ néng bāng wǒ yí ge máng ma 你能帮我一个忙吗？

1219. May I help you?
Wǒ kěyǐ bāngzhù nǐ ma 我可以帮助你吗？

1220. Could you help me?
Nǐ néng bāngzhù wǒ ma 你能帮助我吗？

1221. Would you please give me a hand?
Bāng wǒ ge máng hǎo ma 帮我个忙好吗？

1222. What can I do for you?
Nín xūyào shénme bāngzhù 您需要什么帮助？

1223. Let me help you.
Wǒ lái bāngzhù nǐ 我来帮助你。

1224. HELP!!
Jiù mìng 救命!!

 # Special Occasions

1225. Bless you!
Zhùfù nǐ 祝福你!

1226. Congratulations!
Gōngxǐ gōngxǐ 恭喜恭喜。
- Gōngxǐ 恭喜 is a general term for congratulations. It can be said on a happy occasion such as a wedding, graduation ceremony, the birth of a child, or any other congratulations. Gōngxǐ 恭喜 can be said alone or twice to emphasize its meaning.

1227. Congratulations!
Zhùhè nǐ 祝贺你!
- Zhùhè nǐ 祝贺你 is another common term for congratulations. Since it is a verb, it usually comes with the subject of being congratulated.

1228. Congratulations to you!
Xiàng nǐ zhùhè 向你祝贺!

1229. Good luck!
Zhù nǐ hǎo yùn 祝你好运!

Good Luck!

1230. Thanks. I need it.

Xièxiè, jiè nǐ jíyán 谢谢，借你吉言。

1231. Better luck next time.

Zhù nǐ xià yí cì hǎo yùn 祝你下一次好运。

🎧1232. Have fun!

Wánde kāixīn 玩得开心!
- Dé 得 is used as a particle between the verb wán 玩 (play) and its complement kāixīn 开心 (happy) to indicate result.

1233. Enjoy yourself!

Zhù nǐ wánde kāixīn 祝你玩得开心!
- Add zhù nǐ 祝你 to formally wish someone for something.

🎧1234. Have a nice day.

Zhù nǐ yìtiān guòde yúkuài 祝你一天过得愉快。
- Yúkuài 愉快 means happy, and both yú 愉 and kuài 快 have the same radical "忄" which is 心, meaning heart.

1235. Same to you.

Yě zhù nǐ yúkuài 也祝你愉快!

1236. Have a nice weekend/ vacation/ trip .

Zhù nǐ zhōumò/ jiàqí/ lǔtú yúkuài
祝你周末/假期/旅途愉快!

🎧1237. Have a pleasant trip.

Yílù píng'ān 一路平安。

1238. Have a pleasant journey.

Yílù shùn fēng 一路顺风。
- Shùn 顺 means in the direction of and fēng 风 is wind. Shùnfēng 顺风 means have a favorable wind, which originated

from travel by ship in the old days.

🎧1239. Come and visit our place sometime.
Huānyíng nǐ lái wǒ jiā wánr 欢迎你来我家玩儿。

🎧1240. Happy Birthday!
Zhù nǐ shēngrì kuàilè 祝你生日快乐。

MORE: Happy Birthday Song
Let's sing the happy birthday song in
Chinese. It's the same song as in English.

Happy	Birthday	to	you
zhù 祝 nǐ 你	shēngrì 生日	kuài 快	lè 乐
Happy	Birthday	to	you
zhù 祝 nǐ 你	shēngrì 生日	kuài 快	lè 乐
Happy	Birthday	Dear	xxxx
zhù 祝 nǐ 你	shēngrì 生日	kuài 快	lè 乐
Happy	Birthday	to	you
zhù 祝 nǐ 你	shēngrì 生日	kuài 快	lè 乐

🎧1241. I wish you boundless happiness
and a long, long life.
Shòu bǐ nán shān, fú rú dōng hǎi
寿比南山, 福如东海。

- This is said on birthdays, especially to older
  people. It literally means may your age be as
  the Southern mountain and your happiness as the Eastern seas.

🎧1242. Happy Valentine's Day!
Zhù nǐ qíngrén jié kuàilè
祝你情人节 快乐。

- Nowadays, the western Valentine's day is
  getting popular in China, especially in big
  cities, but China has its own traditional
  Chinese Valentine's day called the Night
  of Sevens Day qī xī 七夕 or Double
  Seven Day, as it falls on the seventh day of the seventh lunar
  month. This day originated from the legend about the love story

between the stars Altair and Vega on a late summer night. Either on western Valentine's Day, or Chinese Valentine's day, you can greet people making this Valentine's wish.

1243. Wish all lovers in the world become families at last!
Zhù tiānxià yǒu qíngrén zhōng chéng juànshǔ
祝天下有情人终成眷属。

- On the Night of Sevens Day, many newspapers, road signs and TV channels in China will carry the blessing, "wish all lovers in the world become families at last". This phrase appears in many books and dramas when there is a love story.

1244. Wish everyone good health!
Zhù dàjiā shēntǐ jiànkāng 祝大家身体健康!

1245. Wish our cooperation is successful!
Zhù wǒmen hézuò chénggōng 祝我们合作成功!

1246. Wish you have a happy marriage.
Bái tóu xié lǎo 白头偕老。
- Literally means live in conjugal bliss to a ripe old age.

1247. Merry Christmas
Shèngdàn jié kuàilè 圣诞节快乐。

 MORE: Christmas
Shèngdàn 圣诞 means the birth of Jesus Christ, and many Christmas related terms start with shèngdàn 圣诞.
Santa Claus : shèngdàn lǎorén 圣诞老人
Christmas Eve: shèngdàn jié qiánxī 圣诞节前夕
　　　　　　　píng'ān yè 平安夜
Christmas present: shèngdàn lǐwù 圣诞礼物
Christmas carol : shèngdàn sònggē 圣诞颂歌
Christmas card: shèngdàn kǎ 圣诞卡
Christmas socks: shèngdàn wà 圣诞袜

MORE: Jingle Bells
Would you like to sing Jingle Bells in Chinese? When singing, tones are ignored.

Líng'ér xiǎng dīngdāng 《铃儿响叮当》

chōngpò dà fēngxuě wǒmen zuòzai xuěqiāo shang
冲破　大风雪　我们　坐在　雪橇　上
(Breaking through a big storm, we are on the sled)

bēnchí guo tiányě huānxiào yòu gēchàng
奔驰　过　田野　欢笑　又　歌唱
(running through the field, happily singing)

líng'ér xiǎng dīngdāng jīngshén duō huānchàng
铃儿　响　叮当　精神　多　欢畅
(jingle bells, how happy spirit)

jīnwǎn huáxuě zhēn kuàile huáxuě gēr chàng
今晚　滑雪　真　快乐　滑雪　歌儿　唱
(tonight skiing is so fun, we are singing about it)

dīngdīng dāng dīngdīng dāng líng'ér xiǎng dīngdāng
叮叮　当　叮叮　当　铃儿　响　叮当
(jingle bells, jingle bells, the bells are jingling)

wǒmen huáxuě duō kuàile huáxuě gēr chàng
我们　滑雪　多　快乐　雪滑　歌儿　唱
(our skiing is so fun, we are singing about it)

1248. Happy New Year!
Xīnnián kuàilè 新年快乐!

- China uses the Gregorian calendar for civil purposes, but New Year's Day follows the lunar calendar. The Chinese Lunar New Year, known as the Spring Festival Chūnjié 春节 (chūn 春 -spring), is the biggest holiday in China. Spring Festival falls on the 1st day of the 1st lunar month, somewhere between late January and mid February. Xīnnián kuàilè 新年快乐 makes a great greeting from New Year's day through the Lantern Festival Yuánxiāo jié 元宵节, which is the 15th day of the first lunar month up until the end of the first lunar month.

🎧1249. Congratulations and be prosperous.
Gōngxǐ fācái 恭喜发财。

- Since New Years is the most important holiday in China, many new years wishes, xīnnián zhùfú yǔ 新年祝福语, are exchanged during the holidays. A monetary gift called hóngbāo 红包 (meaning red packet) is typically given by the grown-ups and seniors to the visiting children and juniors. The recipient will say something auspicious upon taking the red packet.

1250. Be blessed and have profit every year.
Nián nián yǒu yú 年年有余。

- Yú 余 means surplus and it sounds the same as yú 鱼, which means fish. If you have seen the picture of a fish at Chinese restaurants, now you know why. Fish is also included in the New Years Eve dinner for its prosperous symbolism.

1251. Be peaceful every year!
Suì suì píng'ān 岁岁平安。

- Suì 岁 means year, and it has the same meaning as nián 年. Píng'ān 平安 has the same meaning in yílù píng'ān 一路平安 (have a nice trip, or Bon voyage) and in píng'ān yè 平安夜 (Christmas Eve).

1252. Have a prosperous year!
Cáiyuán guǎng jìn 财源广进。

- It literally means have all financial resources coming in.

🎧1253. Wish your dreams come true.
Xīn xiǎng shì chéng 心想事成。

- It iterally means wish whatever you are planning becomes reality. It can be used on New Years or to anyone making a fresh start.

1254. Wish everything is as you wanted.
Wànshì rú yì 万事如意。

1255. Wish all is well.
Wànshì dà jí 万事大吉。

1256. Wish the lucky star shines on you.
Fúxīng gāo zhào 福星高照!

1257. Wish you luck in the year of the Boar!
Zhū nián jíxiáng 猪年吉祥!

 **Signs**

1258. 火警 119
Huǒ jǐng yī yī jiǔ
Fire alarm 119

1259. 请勿吸烟
 Qǐng wū xīyān
No Smoking!

1260. 严禁吸烟
Yǎn jìn xīyān
Absouletely No Smoking!
- This is a lot more serious warning than qǐng wū xīyān 请勿吸烟.

1261. 吸烟有害健康
Xīyān yǒu hài jiànkāng

Smoking is bad for your health.

1262. □□博物馆
Bówùguǎn
□□ Museum

1263. 欢迎参观
Huānyíng cānguān
Visitors are Welcome.

1264. 免费参观
 Miǎnfèi cānguān
Visiters are free.

1265. 谢绝参观
Xièjué cānguān
No Visiters.

1266. 非公莫入
Fēi gōng mò rù
Employees only.

1267. 售票处
Shòu piào chù
Ticketing Office

1268. 凭票入场
Píng piào rù cháng
Admission by tickets only.

1269. 请您排队购票
票款当面点清
Qǐng nín páiduì gòu piào
Piào kuǎn dāngmiàn diǎn qīng
Please line up for purchasing tickets.

Check your tickets and change on the spot.
- This sign is displayed on the window of ticketing offices.

🔊 1270. 请准备□□押金

Qǐng zhǔnbèi □□ yājīn

Please get your deposit ready for □□.
- If you are renting something, most likely a deposit will be required. Renting a boat in an amusement park usually needs up to 300 RMB deposit.

1271. 存包处

Cún bāo chù

Luggage Office
- Many tourist places or buildings don't allow your bags inside. You need to store your bag or big purses in a luggage office. Fees are based on the size of your bag. Leave your big bag in the hotel room!

1272. 小心碰头

Xiǎoxīn pèng tóu

Watch your head.

🔊 1273. 小心路滑

Xiǎoxīn lù huá

Slippery when wet.

1274. 小心油漆

Xiǎoxīn yóu qī

Wet paint.

1275. 古装摄影

Gǔzhuāng shèyǐng

Chinese Clothing photographs
- Many tourist places offer photographs with clothings, background set up, or even with children. Mostly they are not free.

🔊1276. 公共卫生间
Gōnggòng wèishēngjiān
Public toilet

1277. 在您方便后， 请冲水
Zài nín fāngbiàn hòu, qǐng chōng shuǐ
Please flush after use.

🔊1278. 请节约用水
Qǐng jiéyuē yòng shuǐ
Please save water.

🔊1279. 保护环境
Bǎohù huánjìng
Protect the environment.

1280. 足下留青
Zú xià liú qīng
Keep off the grass.
- Literally means leave grass under your feet. This is the made up term from shǒu xià liú qíng 手下留情, which means show your mercy to enemies.

1281. 保持车距
Bǎochí chē jù
Keep distance between cars.

🔊1282. 禁止停车
Jìnzhǐ tíngchē
No Parking.

1283.

Tíng
Stop

1284.

Ràng
Yield

 1285.

<Màn> chēliàng màn xíng
Slow. Reduce Speed.

 1286.

Dàolù fēngbì
Road Closed.

1287.

Fú
Fortune

- This is usually written in black on red paper and hung upside down on the wall or door, so fourtune can "fall" on you.

1288.

招财进宝。
Zhāo cái jìn bǎo
Bring in wealth and treasure.

- If you look closely at this emblem, it actually is the four Traditional characters of **招財進寶** in one.

1289.

Shuāng xǐ
Double happiness.

- This character is commonly used as a decoration, mainly for weddings and marriages. It is two of the characters 喜 put together.

1290.

Chūn	xià	qiū	dōng
Spring	summer	autumn	winter

1291.

Shòu
Longevity

1292.

Cái yuán gǔn gǔn
Wish money keeps rolling in.

 1293.

Guó tài mín ān
Bless the country and the people.
- Read the four characters from left to right, top to bottom 国泰民安. It's a common phrase which appears in many government offices.

1294. □□大厦
Dàxià
□□Building

1295. □□公司
Gōngsī
□□Company

1296. 营业中
Yíngyè zhōng
Open

🎧1297. 营业时间
Yíngyè shíjiān
Business Hours

- Though China spans six time zones, China operates to a single Standard Time (GMT+8) all year round. Most banks, government, and business offices start from 8 am to 5 pm, with around a 2 hour lunch break somewhere between 11:30 and 2 pm. However, daily schedules change both seasonally and from region to region. Shops and restaurants set their own hours as well.

1298. 24 小时
Èr shí sì xiǎoshí
24 hours

🎧1299. □□服务中心
Fúwù zhōngxīn
□□ Service Center

1300. 服务柜台
Fúwù guìtái
Service Counter

1301. □□健身中心
Jiànshēn zhōngxīn
□□ Gym

🎧1302. □□购物中心
Gòuwù zhōngxīn
□□Shopping Center

🎧1303. □□百货大楼
Bǎihuò dàlóu
□□Department Store

🎧1304. □□商场
Shāngcháng
□□Shopping mall

1305. □□商店
Shāngdiàn
□□Shop

🎧1306. 削价清货
拆房动迁
Xiāojià qīnghuò
Chāifáng dòngqiān
Clearance Sale.
Due to moving.

1307. 仅此一场，万勿错过
Jǐn cí yì cháng, wàn wù cuò guò
Only this time, don't miss it.

🎧1308. 全场 1 折起
Quáncháng yī zhé qǐ
Everything from 90% off.

🎧1309. 特价商品
Tè jià shāngpǐn
Special priced items.

🎧1310. 新品上市
Xīn pǐn shàng shì
New Arrival.

1311. 卖完了
Mài wán le
Sold out.

1312. 顾客满意高于一切
Gùkè mǎnyì gāo yú yíqiè
Customer satisfaction is our top priority.

🎧1313. □□餐厅
Cāntīng
□□Restaurant

🎧1314. □□餐馆
Cānguǎn
□□Restaurant

1315. □□餐坊
Cānfáng
□□Restaurant

🎧1316. □□酒家
Jiǔjiā
□□Restaurant

- There is no difference between cāntīng 餐厅, cānguǎn 餐馆, cānfáng 餐坊, and jiǔjiā 酒家. It is up to the individual restaurant to name themselves.

1317. 面点小吃
Miàndiǎn xiǎochī
Noodles and snacks

1318. 火锅
Huǒguō
Hotpot (restaurant)

🎧1319. 外卖
Wài mài
Take out

1320. 香烟
Xiāng yān
Cigarettes

1321. 烟酒
Yān jiǔ
Cigarettes and (alcohol) drinks

🎧1322. □□茶馆
Cháguǎn
□□Tea House

1323. □□茶坊
Cháfáng
□□Tea House

🎧1324. □□酒店
Jiǔdiàn
□□ Hotel

🎧1325. □□大饭店
Dà fàndiàn
□□ Hotel

🎧1326. □□宾馆
Bīn guǎn
□□ Hotel

1327. □□商务酒店
Shāngwù jiǔdiàn
□□ Business Hotel

🎧1328. □□酒吧
Jiǔba

□□ Bar

1329. □□夜总会
Yèzǒnghuì
□□Night Club

1330. 巴士站
Bāshì zhàn
Bus Station

1331. 公车站
Gōngchē zhàn
Bus station

1332. 地铁站
Dìtiě zhàn
Subway Station

1333. 快速冲印
Kuàisù chōngyìn
Fast film processing

1334. 修车
Xiū chē
Bicycle Repair

1335. 打气
Dǎqì
Bike air pump

1336. 配钥匙
Pèi yàoshi
Keys

🎧1337. 上网屋
Shàngwǎng wū
Internet Cafe

1338. 影剧院
Yǐngjù yuàn
Cinema

1339. 出租，出售，房屋
Chūzū, chūshòu, fángwū
Rent, Sell, House (Real Estate Office)

🎧1340. 建设和谐社会
Jiànshè héxié shèhuì
Build a harmonious society
   • These types of slogans are usually found on the walls.

1341. 文明商务区
Wénmíng shāngwù qū
Civilized business area

1342. 文明交通，从我做起
Wénmíng jiāotōng, cóng wǒ zuò qǐ
Civilized traffic starts with me.

1343. 质量责任重于泰山
Zhìliàng zérèn zhòng yú tàishān
Responsibility for quality is most important.
   • Literally means responsibility for quality is heavier than the Tai
     mountain. This slogans appears in factories.

🎧1344. 高高兴兴上班，平平安安回家
 Gāo gāo xìng xìng shàngbān, píng píng ān ān huíjiā
Cheerfully go to work, safely go home.
   • Gāoxìng 高兴 and píng'ān 平安 are repeated for emphasis.

This slogan appears in the offices.

1345. 发展体育运动，增强人民体质
Fāzhǎn tǐyù yùndòng, zēngqiáng rénmín tǐzhì
Promote physical culture and build up the people's health.

1346. 锻炼身体，保卫祖国
Duànliàn shēntǐ, bǎowèi zǔguó
Build up a good physique to defend the country.

 # Common Idioms

1347. Time is money.
Shíjiān jiùshì jīnqián 时间就是金钱。

1348. Knowledge is power.
Zhīshì jiùshì lìliàng 知识就是力量。

1349. No pain，no gain.
Bù láo wú huò 不劳无获。

1350. Easy come, easy go.
Láide róngyì, qùde kuài 来得容易，去得快。

1351. Let bygones be bygones.
Guòqùde, jiù ràng tā guòqù ba
过去的，就让它过去吧。

1352. Another day, another dollar.
Hé wǎngcháng yíyàng 和往常一样。

1353. It's a small world.
Zhè shìjiè zhēn xiǎo 这世界真小。

🎧1354. The wall has ears.
Gé qiāng yǒu ér 隔墙有耳。

🎧1355. As soon as possible!
Jǐnkuài 尽快。

🎧1356. The sooner the better.
Yuè kuài yuè hǎo 越快越好!
- Yuè 越……..yuè 越 means the more……the more.

1357. The more the better.
Yuè duō yuè hǎo 越多越好。

🎧1358. Frankly speaking.
Dǎkāi tiānchuāng shuō liàng huà 打开天窗说亮话。
- Literally means open skylight, talk clearly.

1359. Two heads are better than one.
Rén duō zhì guǎng 人多智广。
- Literally means more people better knowledge.

1360. Hold your horses.
Nài xīn diǎnr 耐心点儿。

🎧1361. Look before you leap.
Sān sī ér hòu xíng 三思而后行。
- Literally means think three times and take action. Ér 而 is a conjunction connecting aim and action.

🎧1362. Nothing is impossible to a willing heart.

Shì shàng wú nán shì, zhǐ pà yǒu xīn rén
世上无难事，只怕有心人。
- Literally means in this world there exists no such impossible tasks, they fear only those with perseverance.

1363. If you keep working, you will have success.
Yǒu zhì zhě shì jìng chéng
有志者事竟成。

🎵1364. The shortest answer is doing.
Zuì jiǎnduǎnde huídá shì gàn 最简短的回答是干。

1365. Clothes make the man.
Rén yào yī zhuāng 人要衣装。

1366. Love me，love my dog.
Ài wū jí wū 爱屋及乌。
- Literally means love for a person extends even to the crows on his roof.

🎵1367. First come first served.
Xiān dào xiān dé 先到先得。

1368. Great minds think alike.
Yīngxióng suǒ jiàn luè tóng 英雄所见略同。

🎵1369. It's better than nothing.
Zǒng bǐ méiyǒu hǎo 总比没有好。

1370. Kill two birds with one stone.
Yì jǔ liǎng dé 一举两得。Or, Yì shí èr niǎo 一石二鸟。
- To describe a plan, idea, action, or method which can achieve two goals.

🎧 1371. That's always the case.
Xí yǐ wéi cháng 习以为常。

🎧 1372. Just in case.
Yǐ fǎng wàn yī 以防万一。

1373. It's a once in a lifetime chance.
Zhè shì yìshēng nándéde jīhuì 这是一生难得的机会。

🎧 1374. Beauty is in the eye of the beholder.
Qíngrén yǎnli chū Xīshī
情人眼里出西施。

- Literally means "Xīshī 西施" is in lover's eyes.
  Xīshī 西施 (506BC~?) was one of the Four
  Beauties in ancient China. Dazzled by her beauty, fish stopped
  swimming and sunk to the bottom of the river, while condors
  stopped flying and fell to the ground. She was from the State of
  Yue, and was sent to the king of the State of Wu as a gift. The
  King was so indulged in his love with her he forgot all about
  his state affairs. The State of Yue finally got its revenge.

1375. Carry the thing through, whatever the consequences.
Yì bú zuò, èr bù xiū 一不做，二不休。
- What we have started we will pursue to the end at any cost.

1376. Build up from nothing.
Bái shǒu qǐ jiā 白手起家。

🎧 1377. Out of sight, out of mind
Yǎn bú jiàn, xīn bù xiǎng 眼不见, 心不想。

1378. Ladies first.
Nǚshì yōuxiān 女士优先。

🎧 1379. To have really given much thought to the matter.
Yòngxīn liángkǔ 用心良苦。

🎵1380. Refuse nobody, go after nobody.
Láizhě bú jù, qùzhě bù zhuī 來者不拒, 去者不追。

1381. Come and go as you wish.
Xiǎng lái jiù lái, xiǎng qù jiù qù 想來就來, 想去就去。

🎵1382. A fox may grow grey, but never good. A leopard cannot change his spots.
Jiāng shān yì gǎi, běnxìng nán yí 江山易改, 本性难移。
- It's easy to change rivers and mountains but hard to alter a person's nature.

1383. From saying to doing is a long step.
Shuōzhe róngyì, zuòzhe nán 说着容易, 做着难。

🎵1384. Good will be rewarded with good, and evil with evil.
Shàn yǒu shàn bào, è yǒu è bào
善有善报, 恶有恶报。

🎵1385. It varies from person to person.
Yīn rén ér yì 因人而異。

🎵1386. Different people, different views.
Jiàn rén jiàn zhì 见仁见智。

🎵1387. Look for a flaw where there is none.
Jīdànli tiāo gǔtóu 鸡蛋里挑骨头。
- Literally means picking bones from an egg.

1388. There is no concealing the truth.-The truth will come out!
Zhǐ bāo bú zhù huǒ 纸包不住火。
- Literally means you can't wrap fire in paper. Zhù

住 is used after a verb as a complement indicating a halt, standstill etc.

🎧1389. An eye for an eye, a tooth for a tooth.
Yǐ yǎn huán yǎn, yǐ yá huán yá 以眼还眼, 以牙还牙。
- Treat your enemies as how they treated you.

🎧1390. The spectator sees the game better than the players.
Dān jú zhě mí, páng guān zhě qīng
当局者迷，旁观者清。
- Men are blind in their own cause.

1391. Good teachers make good students.
Míngshī chū gāo tú 名师出高徒。

1392. Win honors for the motherland.
Wèi zǔguó zhēngguāng 为祖国争光。

1393. Do not be dizzy with success, nor discouraged by defeat.
Shèng bù jiāo, bài bù něi 胜不骄，败不馁。

1394. Up to one's best level in skill and style of play.
Dǎ chū shuǐpíng , dǎ chū fēnggé 打出水平，打出风格。

🎧1395. When there is life, there is hope.
Liúde qīng shān zài, bú pà méi chái shāo
留得青山在，不怕没柴烧。
- Literally means when there is still Qing mountain, no need to worry about firewood to burn.

🎧1396. Gilding the lily.
Huà shé tiān zú 画蛇添足。
- It literally means adding legs when painting a snake. Don't ruin your work by an unnecessary addition.

1397. Worry about petty gain or loss.
Jǐnjīn jìjiào 斤斤计较。

1398. As good as assured.
Shíná jiǔwěn 十拿九稳。
- Literally means you hold ten, nine is safe.

🎧1399. Be perfectly happy too.
Xīngān qíngyuàn 心甘情愿。

1400. Failure is the mother of success.
Shībài nǎi chénggōng zhī mǔ 失败乃成功之母。
- It is not a problem to taste failure. One can learn from his/her mistakes and thus make failure become a success.

1401. Never employ the man you suspect, nor suspect the man you employ.
Yí rén mò yòng, yòng rén mò yí
疑人莫用，用人莫疑。

🎧1402. A friend in need is a friend indeed. Adversity allows one to see the true feelings of others.
Huànnàn jiàn zhēnqíng 患难见真情。

🎧1403. At birth we bring nothing; at death we take away nothing.
Shēng bú dài lái, sǐ bú dài qù 生不带来，死不带去。

1404. You can not open a book without learning something. Reading is always profitable.
Kāijuàn yǒuyì 开卷有益。

Appendix-2008 Beijing Olympics

1405. The 2008 Olympic Games will be held in Beijing China.

Èr líng líng bā nián Àoyùnhuì zài Zhōngguó Běijīng jǔbàn

2008 年奥运会在中国北京举办。

- Àoyùnhuì 奥运会 is the shortened name of Àolínpǐkè Yùndò nghuì 奥林匹克运动会.

1406. The International Olympic Committee constituted itself on 23rd June 1894.

Guójì Àowěihuì yú yī bā jiǔ sì nián liù yuè èr shí sān rì chénglì

国际奥委会于 1894 年 6 月 23 日成立。

1407. The official languages of the IOC are French and English.

Guójì Àowěihuìde guānfāng yǔyán shì Fǎyǔ hé Yīngyǔ

国际奥委会的官方语言是法语和英语。

1408. The motto of the 2008 Olympics is "One World, One Dream".

Èr líng líng bā Àoyùnhuìde zhǔtí kǒuhào shì tóng yī ge shìjiè, tóng yī ge mèngxiǎng

2008 奥运会的主题口号是"同一个世界同一个梦想"。

1409. The opening ceremony is on Aug 8th 2008.

Kāimù shì zài èr líng líng bā nián bā yuè bā hào jǔxíng

开幕式在 2008 年 8 月 8 号举行。

- Closing ceremony bìmù shì 闭幕式.

1410. The Olympic Games shall be proclaimed open by the Head of State of the host country.
Àoyùnhuì yóu dōngdào guó guójiā yuánshǒu xuānbù kāimù
奥运会由东道国国家元首宣布开幕。

1411. Fuwa are the mascots of the 2008 Summer Olympics in Beijing.
Fúwá shì èr líng líng bā nián Běijīng Àoyùnhuìde jíxiángwù
福娃是 2008 年北京奥会运的吉祥物。

1412. Besides Beijing, there are 5 other venues: Qingdao, Hong Kong, Tianjin, Shanghai, and Qinhuangdao.
Chúle Běijīng yǐwài, háiyou wǔ ge huìcháng: Qīngdǎo, Xiānggǎng, Tiānjīn, Shànghǎi hé Qínhuángdǎo
除了北京以外, 还有 5 个 会场: 青岛,香港, 天津, 上海和秦皇岛。

1413. The Olympic symbol is the five interlocking rings.
Àolínpǐkède biāozhì shì wǔ ge xiāngliánde yuánhuán
奥林匹克的标志是五个相连的圆环。

1414. It represents the union of the five continents and the meeting of the athletes of the world at the Olympic Games.
Tā dàibiǎozhe wùdàzhōude tuánjié hé quán shìjiè yùndòngyuán zài Àoyùnhuìshang xiāngjù yì táng
它代表着五大洲的团结和全世界运动员在奥运会上相聚一堂。

1415. The Olympic flame is a symbol reminiscent of the ancient Olympic Games.
Àoyùn shènghuǒ shì rénmen miǎnhuái gǔdài Àoyùnhuìde xiàngzhèng

奥运圣火是人们缅怀古代奥运会的象征。

- Olympic torch is Àoyùn huǒjù 奥运火炬.

1416. The Olympic Games consist of the Games of the Olympiad and the Olympic Winter Games.
Àoyùnhuì bāokuò xiàjì Àoyùnhuì hé dōngjì Àoyùnhuì
奥运会包括夏季奥运会和冬季奥运会。

Both take place every four years.
Tāmen dōushì méi sì nián jǔbàn yí cì
它们都是每四年举办一次。

1417. The Olympic delegation parade is in alphabetical order according to the language of the host country.
Àoyùnhuì dàibiǎotuán àn dōngdào guó yǔyán wénzide zìmǔ shùnxù rùcháng
奥运会代表团按东道国语言文字的字母顺序入场。

1418. Greece and the host country are exceptions.
Xīlà hé dōngdào guó shì lìwài 希腊和东道国是例外。

1419. Greece leads the parade, and the host country brings up the rear.
Xīlà dàibiǎotuán dì yíge rùcháng, dōngdào guó dàibiǎotuán zuì hòu yí ge rùcháng
希腊代表团第一个入场，东道国代表团最后一个入场。

1420. Humanistic Olympics.
Rénwén Àoyùn 人文奥运

1421. Olympic Anthem.
Àoyùnhuì huìgē 奥运会会歌

1422. Olympic village.

Àoyùn cūn 奥运村

1423. Organization committee.
Zǔwěihuì 组委会

1424. Rewrite the world record.
Shuáxīn shìjiè jìlù 刷新世界记录

1425. Establish a record
Chuàng jìlù 创记录

1426. World-record holder
Shìjiè jìlù bǎochízhe 世界纪录保持者

1427. Gain world championship
Dé guànjūn 得冠军
- Champion or gold medalist: guànjūn 冠军
- All-round champion: quánnéng guànjūn 全能冠军
- Silver medalist:yàjūn 亚军
- Bronze medalist: dìsānmíng 第三名
- Podium: bānjiǎngtái 颁奖台

1428. Dark horse
Hēimǎ 黑马
- Favorite: kěwàng qǔshèngzhe 可望取胜者
- Outsider: wú qǔshèng xīwàngzhe 无取胜希望者

1429. Event
Xiàngmù 项目
- Team event : tuántǐ xiàngmù 团体项目
- Individual event: dānrén xiàngmù 单人项目
- Men's event: nánzi xiàngmù男子项目
- Women's event: nǚzi xiàngmù 女子项目

1430. Heavyweight

Zhòngliáng jí 重量级
- Middleweight: zhōngliáng jí 中量级
- Lightweight: qīngliáng jí 轻量级

1431. Final match.
Juésài 决赛
- Preliminary match: yùsài 预赛
- Draw: chōuqiān 抽签
- Eighth-final: bā fēn zhī yī juésài 八分之一决赛
- Quarterfinal: sì fēn zhī yī juésài 四分之一决赛
- Semi-final: bàn juésài 半决赛
- Elimination match: táotài sài 淘汰赛

1432. Competition regulations.
Bǐsài tiáolì 比赛条例
- Doping test: yàojiǎn 药检
- Disqialification: qǔxiāo bǐsài zīgé 取消比赛资格
- Match ban: jìnsài mìnglìng 禁赛命令
- Send a player off: pànfá chūcháng 判罚出场
- Red card: hóngpái 红牌
- Yellow card: huángpái 黄牌

1433. Spectator
Guānzhòng 观众
- Sports fan: yùndòng àihàozhe 运动爱好者
- Cheerleader: lā lā duì 啦啦队
- Coach: jiàoliànyuán 教练员

1434. Olympic Game List
Àoyùnhuì bǐsài xiàngmù 奥运会比赛项目

Archery: shèjiàn 射箭
Athletics/track & field: tiánjìng 田径
Badminton: yǔmáoqiú 羽毛球
Baseball: bàngqiú 棒球
Basketball: lánqiú 篮球

Boxing: quánjí 拳击
Canoeing: huátǐng 滑艇
Cycling: zìxíngchē yùndòng 自行车运动
Diving competition: tiàoshuǐ 跳水
Equestrian: qímǎ 骑马
Fencing: jíjiàn 击剑
football/soccer: zúqiú 足球
Hockey: qūgùnqiú 曲棍球
Gymnastics: tǐcāo 体操
Handball: shǒuqiú 手球
Judo: róudào 柔道
Marathon (race): mǎlāsōng sàipǎo 马拉松赛跑
Modern pentathlon: xiàndài wǔxiàng yùndòng
现代五项运动
Rowing: huáchuán 划船
Sailing: fānchuán 帆船
Shooting: shèjí 射击
Softball: lěiqiú 垒球
Swimming: yóuyǒng 游泳
Table tennis: pīngpāngqiú 乒乓球
Taekwondo: táiquándào 跆拳道
Tennis: wǎngqiú 网球
Triathlon: tiěrén sānxiàng 铁人三项
Volleyball: páiqiú 排球
Water polo: shuǐqiú 水球
Weightlifting: jǔzhòng 举重
Wrestling: shuāijiāo 摔交

Appendix-Family Members

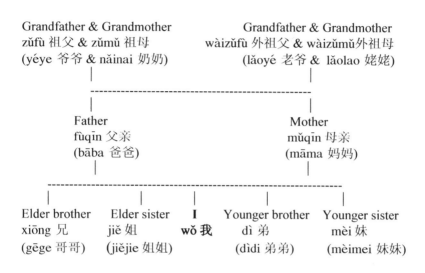

Grandfather & Grandmother
zǔfù 祖父 & zǔmǔ 祖母
(yéye 爷爷 & nǎinai 奶奶)

Grandfather & Grandmother
wàizǔfù 外祖父 & wàizǔmǔ外祖母
(lǎoyé 老爷 & lǎolao 姥姥)

Father
fùqīn 父亲
(bāba 爸爸)

Mother
mǔqīn 母亲
(māma 妈妈)

Elder brother
xiōng 兄
(gēge 哥哥)

Elder sister
jiě 姐
(jiějie 姐姐)

I
wǒ 我

Younger brother
dì 弟
(dìdi 弟弟)

Younger sister
mèi 妹
(mèimei 妹妹)

Husband
zhàngfu 丈夫

Wife
qīzi 妻子

Son & Daughter-in-law
érzi 儿子 & érxífur 儿媳妇儿

Daughter & Son-in-law
nǚ'ér 女儿 & nǚxu 女婿

Grandson
sūnzi 孙子

Granddaughter
sūnnǚ 孙女

Grandson
wàisūn 外孙

Granddaughter
wàisūnnǚ 外孙女

The ones in ( ) are colloquial. Husband and wife are called
zhàngfu 丈夫 and qīzi 妻子, and address each other as

àirén 愛人 in mainland China. Taiwan also use zhàngfu 丈夫 and qīzi 妻子 as well as xiānsheng 先生 and tàitai 太太 for husband and wife. You may notice the titles of grandchildren are different based on whether they are from a son or daughter. Wài 外 originally means outside and here it means relatives of one's mother, sister, or daughter. As you can see, 女 is a radical for most female family member names. Chinese titles of address between relatives are based on relationship, gender, and age. Below is for your reference, and gives an example of the complex system of family titles. If you begin with "Me", each individual family member has their own address.

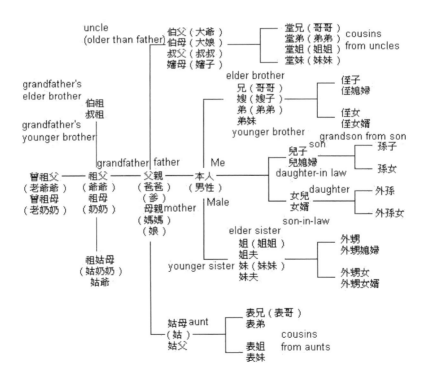

Made in the USA